'Put On the New Person'

CHRISTIAN
PUBLISHING HOUSE

PUT OFF THE OLD PERSON

Edward D. Andrews

SECOND EDITION

PUT OFF THE OLD PERSON

Put On the New Person

Second Edition

Edward D. Andrews

Christian Publishing House
Cambridge, Ohio

Copyright © 2016, 2024 Edward D. Andrews

All rights reserved. Except for brief quotations in articles, other publications, book reviews, and blogs, no part of this book may be reproduced in any manner without prior written permission from the publishers. For information, write, support@christianpublishers.org

PUT OFF THE OLD PERSON: Put On the New Person by Edward D. Andrews

ISBN-13: **978-1-945757-18-1**

ISBN-10: **1-945757-18-3**

Table of Contents

Preface 6

Introduction 8

CHAPTER 1 How Deeply Are We Affected by Our Human Imperfection? 10

CHAPTER 2 How Can We Win the Battle for the Mind? . 18

CHAPTER 3 How Can We Be Biblically Minded? 28

CHAPTER 4 How Can the Renewal of Your Mind Transform Your Life? 41

CHAPTER 5 How Can We Keep the Mind Renewed? 55

CHAPTER 6 How Can We Walk in the Light from God? 69

CHAPTER 7 What Is the Mind of Christ? 79

CHAPTER 8 How Can We Address Spiritual Sicknesses of Mind and Heart? 90

CHAPTER 9 How Can We Develop the Right Desires? . 101

CHAPTER 10 How Can We Cope with Life's Problems Through God's Guidance? 112

CHAPTER 11 How Can We Distinguish Right from Wrong in a World of Moral Confusion? 120

CHAPTER 12 How Can We Walk in Integrity and Uphold Moral Standards in Every Aspect of Our Lives? 126

CHAPTER 13 How Can We Build a Successful and Godly Family Life? 134

Edward D. Andrews

Preface

The Christian life is often described as a journey—a journey that begins with the recognition of our fallen nature and continues with the daily endeavor to conform to the image of Christ. This book, *Put Off the Old Person: Put On the New Person [Second Edition]*, is not just a guidebook for this journey, but a call to arms for every believer who desires to live a life that honors Jehovah.

The first edition of this book was born out of a deep conviction that many Christians today struggle with the practical aspects of spiritual growth. While the foundational truths of the faith are well-known, the application of these truths in daily life often remains a challenge. This second edition aims to build on the foundation laid by the first, offering even more practical insights, scriptural reflections, and actionable steps to help believers navigate the complexities of modern life while staying true to the principles of Scripture.

As I revisited the content for this second edition, I was struck by the enduring relevance of the topics covered. The issues that believers face today—whether they pertain to personal integrity, family life, or the battle against sin—are not new. They are the same struggles that Christians have faced for centuries. Yet, in our rapidly changing world, these challenges can feel more pressing, more complex, and at times, more overwhelming. This edition seeks to address these concerns with greater depth and clarity, providing a resource that is both timeless and timely.

One of the key themes that runs throughout this book is the idea of intentionality. Spiritual growth does not happen by accident. It requires deliberate effort, guided by the wisdom of Scripture and empowered by the grace of God. This book is designed to help you cultivate that intentionality in every area of your life. Whether you are seeking to strengthen your family relationships, develop godly desires, or simply live a life of integrity, this book provides the tools and insights you need to make meaningful progress.

I have also made a conscious effort in this edition to emphasize the importance of practical application. It is one thing to know what the Bible says about a particular issue; it is another thing entirely to live it out. My hope is that the reflections, examples, and strategies offered in these pages will not only deepen your understanding but also inspire you to take concrete steps toward spiritual maturity.

As you embark on this journey of transformation, I encourage you to approach it with an open heart and a willing spirit. Be prepared to challenge yourself, to confront areas of your life that may need change, and to trust in Jehovah's guidance every step of the way. The process of putting off the old person and putting on the new is not easy, but it is the path to true freedom, joy, and fulfillment in Christ.

I am grateful for the opportunity to share this journey with you through this book. It is my prayer that Jehovah will use these pages to draw you closer to Him, to strengthen your faith, and to equip you for every good work.

May you be blessed as you pursue the calling to which you have been called.

Edward D. Andrews

Author of 220+ books and Chief Translator of the Updated American Standard Version (UASV)

Edward D. Andrews

Introduction

The journey of transformation in the Christian life is one that demands more than a superficial adjustment; it calls for a profound renewal of the heart, mind, and soul. In *Put Off the Old Person: Put On the New Person*, we delve into the essence of this transformation, exploring what it truly means to shed the old self, marred by sin and imperfection, and to embrace the new person, fashioned in the likeness of Christ.

Human imperfection is not merely an external blemish; it is a deeply rooted condition that affects every aspect of our being. From the very beginning, when Adam and Eve first transgressed Jehovah's command, humanity has been battling the consequences of sin—a battle that takes place primarily in the mind and heart. The Scriptures clearly reveal that this internal struggle is not only a matter of occasional lapses but an ongoing conflict between the old, corrupt nature and the new, renewed spirit that believers are called to adopt.

This book is an invitation to engage deeply with the truths of Scripture, to confront the reality of our human imperfection, and to actively participate in the process of spiritual renewal. It is not enough to acknowledge our fallen state; we must be willing to take practical, actionable steps to align our lives with God's will. Through the guidance of the Spirit-inspired Word of God, we are called to develop the right desires, cope with life's problems in a godly manner, and distinguish between right and wrong in a world increasingly characterized by moral confusion.

Moreover, this book emphasizes the importance of family life as a cornerstone of Christian living. Success in family life is not an accident but the result of intentional effort and a commitment to living according to biblical principles. By appreciating our roles within the family, fostering communication, and practicing forgiveness, we can build a family life that reflects the love and grace of God.

As you read through the chapters of this book, you will find that the path to spiritual renewal is both challenging and rewarding. It requires discipline, humility, and above all, a steadfast reliance on God's grace. The process of putting off the old person and putting on the new is not a one-time event but a lifelong journey that demands ongoing vigilance and perseverance.

This book does not offer quick fixes or easy solutions. Instead, it provides a thorough and biblically grounded exploration of what it means to live a life transformed by the power of God's Word. It is my hope and prayer that as you engage with the teachings in this book, you will be encouraged, equipped, and empowered to continue your journey of spiritual renewal with greater clarity and purpose.

CHAPTER 1 How Deeply Are We Affected by Our Human Imperfection?

Mentally Bent Toward Evil

Human imperfection is a reality that permeates every aspect of our existence. From the moment Adam and Eve disobeyed Jehovah's command, sin entered the world, corrupting the nature of humanity and creating a natural inclination toward evil. Genesis 6:5 underscores this inherent bent, stating, "Jehovah saw that the wickedness of man was great in the earth, and that every intention of the thoughts of his heart was only evil continually." This scripture reveals that the fall did not merely introduce sin as an external influence but corrupted the very core of human nature.

Understanding this inherent inclination toward evil is crucial in our journey to put off the old person and put on the new. It is not enough to acknowledge occasional lapses in judgment; we must recognize that our very nature is flawed. Paul expresses this struggle in Romans 7:21-23, "So I find it to be a law that when I want to do right, evil lies close at hand. For I delight in the law of God, in my inner being, but I see in my members another law waging war against the law of my mind and making me captive to the law of sin that dwells in my members."

This passage illustrates the constant battle between the desire to do good and the persistent presence of evil within us. This struggle is a direct result of the original sin that has been passed down through generations. It is not merely an external temptation but an internal battle that requires ongoing vigilance and reliance on God's Word.

An Unknowable Treacherous Heart

The Bible provides a sobering assessment of the human heart, describing it as deceitful and wicked beyond understanding. In Jeremiah 17:9, we read, "The heart is deceitful above all things, and desperately sick; who can understand it?" This verse captures the essence of human imperfection, emphasizing that our hearts are not only flawed but fundamentally treacherous.

This treachery of the heart is not easily recognized by those who are unaware of their fallen condition. Proverbs 14:12 warns, "There is a way that seems right to a man, but its end is the way to death." This verse highlights the danger of relying on our own understanding and the deceptive nature of our hearts. We may believe that we are on the right path, but without the guidance of Scripture, we are easily led astray.

The unknowable nature of the heart means that self-reliance is a dangerous path. We must continually seek God's wisdom to discern the true state of our hearts. Hebrews 4:12 reminds us, "For the word of God is living and active, sharper than any two-edged sword, piercing to the division of soul and of spirit, of joints and of marrow, and discerning the thoughts and intentions of the heart." Only through the Word of God can we truly understand the depth of our imperfection and begin the process of transformation.

Ignorance of Your Fallen Condition

One of the most pervasive issues in understanding human imperfection is the widespread ignorance of our fallen condition. Many individuals are unaware of the extent to which sin has corrupted their nature. Ephesians 4:18-19 speaks to this ignorance: "They are darkened in their understanding, alienated from the life of God because of the ignorance that is in them, due to their hardness of heart. They have become callous and have given themselves up to sensuality, greedy to practice every kind of impurity."

This ignorance is not merely a lack of knowledge but a willful blindness to the truth of our fallen state. The hardness of heart that accompanies this ignorance leads to a callousness that further alienates us from God. Romans 3:11-12 reinforces this idea, stating, "None is righteous, no, not one; no one understands; no one seeks for God. All have turned aside; together they have become worthless; no one does good, not even one."

The ignorance of our fallen condition is a barrier to spiritual growth. Without a clear understanding of our need for redemption, we cannot fully appreciate the sacrifice of Christ or the power of the Gospel. John 3:19-20 explains, "And this is the judgment: the light has come into the world, and people loved the darkness rather than the light because their works were evil. For everyone who does wicked things hates the light and does not come to the light, lest his works should be exposed."

To overcome this ignorance, we must be willing to confront the darkness within us and seek the light of God's truth. Proverbs 1:7 declares, "The fear of Jehovah is the beginning of knowledge; fools despise wisdom and instruction." By acknowledging our fallen condition and seeking wisdom from the Scriptures, we can begin the journey toward spiritual renewal.

The Conflict of Two Natures

The conflict between the old and new natures is a central theme in the Christian life. As believers, we are constantly torn between the desires of the flesh and the call of the Spirit. This internal struggle is a direct result of our fallen nature, which continues to exert influence even after we have been born again.

Paul describes this conflict in Galatians 5:17, "For the desires of the flesh are against the Spirit, and the desires of the Spirit are against the flesh, for these are opposed to each other, to keep you from doing the things you want to do." This verse highlights the ongoing battle between the two natures within us. While we desire to do good, the flesh continually pulls us toward sin.

The conflict between the old and new natures is not a sign of spiritual failure but a natural part of the Christian experience. Romans 8:7-8 further explains, "For the mind that is set on the flesh is hostile to God, for it does not submit to God's law; indeed, it cannot. Those who are in the flesh cannot please God." This passage emphasizes that as long as we are in the flesh, we will struggle with sin.

However, the presence of this conflict does not mean that we are doomed to failure. Through the power of the Holy Spirit, we can overcome the desires of the flesh and live according to the Spirit. Romans 8:12-13 encourages us, "So then, brothers, we are debtors, not to the flesh, to live according to the flesh. For if you live according to the flesh, you will die, but if by the Spirit you put to death the deeds of the body, you will live."

The key to victory in this conflict lies in our willingness to submit to the Spirit and resist the temptations of the flesh. James 4:7 advises, "Submit yourselves therefore to God. Resist the devil, and he will flee from you." By surrendering to God's will and actively resisting the influence of the flesh, we can experience the transformative power of the Spirit in our lives.

The Father of Evil

The concept of evil is not merely an abstract idea but a reality that has a personal source: Satan, the father of lies. Jesus clearly identifies Satan as the origin of evil in John 8:44, "You are of your father the devil, and your will is to do your father's desires. He was a murderer from the beginning, and does not stand in the truth, because there is no truth in him. When he lies, he speaks out of his own character, for he is a liar and the father of lies."

Satan's role as the father of evil means that he is constantly working to deceive and destroy. His influence is pervasive, affecting every aspect of human life. Ephesians 2:2 describes him as "the prince of the power of the air, the spirit that is now at work in the sons of disobedience." This verse highlights the fact that Satan's influence extends beyond individual temptation to encompass entire systems and cultures.

Recognizing Satan as the father of evil is crucial in understanding the depth of our human imperfection. Our struggles are not merely against flesh and blood but against the spiritual forces of evil in the heavenly places (Ephesians 6:12). This understanding should lead us to a greater awareness of the spiritual battle that we are engaged in and the need for God's protection and guidance.

To resist the influence of Satan, we must be vigilant and steadfast in our faith. 1 Peter 5:8-9 warns, "Be sober-minded; be watchful. Your adversary the devil prowls around like a roaring lion, seeking someone to devour. Resist him, firm in your faith, knowing that the same kinds of suffering are being experienced by your brotherhood throughout the world." By standing firm in our faith and relying on God's strength, we can overcome the schemes of the devil and remain faithful to God's calling.

Controlling Your Mental Bent Toward Evil

Given the depth of our imperfection and the influence of Satan, controlling our mental bent toward evil is a critical aspect of putting off the old person. This process begins with the recognition that our thoughts and desires are often aligned with the flesh rather than the Spirit. Romans 8:5-6 explains, "For those who live according to the flesh set their minds on the things of the flesh, but those who live according to the Spirit set their minds on the things of the Spirit. For to set the mind on the flesh is death, but to set the mind on the Spirit is life and peace."

Controlling our mental bent toward evil requires a deliberate effort to renew our minds. Romans 12:2 instructs, "Do not be conformed to this world, but be transformed by the renewal of your mind, that by testing you may discern what is the will of God, what is good and acceptable and perfect." This renewal of the mind involves a conscious decision to reject the patterns of the world and embrace the values of the Kingdom of God.

One of the most effective ways to control our mental bent toward evil is through the discipline of prayer and meditation on God's Word. Philippians 4:8 advises, "Finally, brothers, whatever is true, whatever is honorable, whatever is just, whatever is pure, whatever is lovely, whatever is commendable, if there is any excellence, if there is anything worthy of praise, think about these things." By filling our minds with the truth of Scripture, we can counteract the lies of the enemy and align our thoughts with God's will.

Another important aspect of controlling our mental bent toward evil is the practice of self-examination. 2 Corinthians 13:5 encourages, "Examine yourselves, to see whether you are in the faith. Test yourselves. Or do you not realize this about yourselves, that Jesus Christ is in you?—unless indeed you fail to meet the test!" Regular self-examination helps us identify areas where we may be allowing sinful thoughts to take root and provides an opportunity to repent and seek God's forgiveness.

There Will Come a Day When Evil Will Be No More

While the struggle against evil is a present reality, Scripture assures us that there will come a day when evil will be no more. This promise is a source of great hope for believers as we navigate the challenges of living in a fallen world. Revelation 21:4 declares, "He will wipe away every tear from their eyes, and death shall be no more, neither shall there be mourning, nor crying, nor pain anymore, for the former things have passed away."

The ultimate defeat of evil is assured through the victory of Christ. Colossians 2:15 states, "He disarmed the rulers and authorities and put them to open shame, by triumphing over them in him." This victory was accomplished through Christ's death and resurrection, which secured the defeat of Satan and the forces of evil. Although we still experience the effects of evil in this present age, we can rest in the knowledge that its power has been broken and its ultimate end is certain.

The anticipation of the day when evil will be no more should motivate us to persevere in our faith and continue the work of putting off the old person and putting on the new. 1 Corinthians 15:58 encourages, "Therefore, my beloved brothers, be steadfast, immovable, always abounding in the work of the Lord, knowing that in the Lord your labor is not in vain." As we strive to live according to

God's will, we do so with the confidence that our efforts will bear fruit in the coming Kingdom.

Christ's Judgment on the Disobedient

While the promise of the end of evil brings hope, it also carries a sobering reminder of the reality of Christ's judgment on the disobedient. The Bible is clear that those who persist in their rebellion against God will face judgment. 2 Thessalonians 1:8-9 warns, "In flaming fire, inflicting vengeance on those who do not know God and on those who do not obey the gospel of our Lord Jesus. They will suffer the punishment of eternal destruction, away from the presence of the Lord and from the glory of his might."

This judgment is not arbitrary but is based on God's perfect justice. Romans 2:6-8 explains, "He will render to each one according to his works: to those who by patience in well-doing seek for glory and honor and immortality, he will give eternal life; but for those who are self-seeking and do not obey the truth, but obey unrighteousness, there will be wrath and fury."

Understanding the reality of Christ's judgment should lead us to a deeper sense of reverence for God and a greater commitment to living in obedience to His Word. Hebrews 10:26-27 offers a stark warning: "For if we go on sinning deliberately after receiving the knowledge of the truth, there no longer remains a sacrifice for sins, but a fearful expectation of judgment, and a fury of fire that will consume the adversaries."

This knowledge should also compel us to share the Gospel with others, warning them of the consequences of rejecting Christ and urging them to turn to Him for salvation. 2 Corinthians 5:11 states, "Therefore, knowing the fear of the Lord, we persuade others. But what we are is known to God, and I hope it is known also to your conscience."

Ongoing Conflict Within Us

As long as we live in this fallen world, the conflict within us between the old and new natures will continue. This ongoing struggle is a reminder of the reality of human imperfection and the need for continual reliance on God's grace. Philippians 3:12-14 captures this tension: "Not that I have already obtained this or am already perfect, but I press on to make it my own, because Christ Jesus has made me his own. Brothers, I do not consider that I have made it my own. But one thing I do: forgetting what lies behind and straining forward to what lies ahead, I press on toward the goal for the prize of the upward call of God in Christ Jesus."

This passage reflects the perseverance required to continue in the faith despite the ongoing conflict. It acknowledges that perfection is not yet attainable in this life but encourages believers to press on toward the goal of Christlikeness.

Romans 7:24-25 also speaks to this conflict: "Wretched man that I am! Who will deliver me from this body of death? Thanks be to God through Jesus Christ our Lord! So then, I myself serve the law of God with my mind, but with my flesh I serve the law of sin." This verse highlights the tension between the desire to serve God and the reality of sin that still resides in our flesh.

The ongoing conflict within us is not a cause for despair but an opportunity to grow in faith and dependence on God. 2 Corinthians 12:9-10 reminds us, "But he said to me, 'My grace is sufficient for you, for my power is made perfect in weakness.' Therefore I will boast all the more gladly of my weaknesses, so that the power of Christ may rest upon me. For the sake of Christ, then, I am content with weaknesses, insults, hardships, persecutions, and calamities. For when I am weak, then I am strong."

Through this conflict, we learn to rely on God's strength rather than our own and to trust in His grace to carry us through. As we continue to put off the old person and put on the new, we can do so with the assurance that God is at work in us, transforming us into the image of His Son.

Edward D. Andrews

CHAPTER 2 How Can We Win the Battle for the Mind?

The Beginning of the Battle for the Mind

The mind is the battleground where the greatest spiritual conflicts are fought. From the very beginning, Satan has targeted the minds of individuals, seeking to lead them away from the truth and into deception. The first recorded instance of this battle occurred in the Garden of Eden, where Satan, through the serpent, questioned and distorted Jehovah's command to Adam and Eve. Genesis 3:1 records Satan's cunning question to Eve: "Did God actually say, 'You shall not eat of any tree in the garden'?" This question planted doubt in Eve's mind, ultimately leading to her and Adam's disobedience.

This initial battle for the mind set the stage for the ongoing spiritual warfare that every human being faces. Satan's strategy has always been to attack the mind, because if he can control a person's thoughts, he can influence their actions. Proverbs 23:7 states, "For as he thinketh in his heart, so is he." This emphasizes the truth that our thoughts shape who we are and determine our behavior.

The battle for the mind is a daily struggle, one that requires vigilance and intentional effort to guard against the enemy's tactics. Ephesians 6:11-12 reminds us, "Put on the whole armor of God, that you may be able to stand against the schemes of the devil. For we do not wrestle against flesh and blood, but against the rulers, against the authorities, against the cosmic powers over this present darkness, against the spiritual forces of evil in the heavenly places." The mind, being the control center of our actions and decisions, is where this spiritual warfare is most fiercely contested.

How to Strengthen Your Mind: Cultivate Your Conscience

One of the most important aspects of winning the battle for the mind is cultivating a strong and sensitive conscience. The conscience, as defined by Scripture, is the internal mechanism that discerns right from wrong, prompting us toward righteous behavior and warning us against sin. Romans 2:15 describes the conscience as bearing witness, "their conscience also bearing witness, and their thoughts the meanwhile accusing or else excusing one another."

A well-cultivated conscience aligns with God's Word and is essential for making sound decisions in the face of temptation. However, a conscience that is ignored or seared by repeated sin can lead to spiritual downfall. Paul warns Timothy about this danger in 1 Timothy 4:2, where he speaks of those "whose consciences are seared as with a hot iron." A seared conscience is one that has been desensitized to sin, no longer feeling the weight of guilt or the need for repentance.

To strengthen the mind and cultivate the conscience, it is essential to immerse oneself in Scripture. Psalm 119:11 declares, "I have stored up your word in my heart, that I might not sin against you." Regular study and meditation on God's Word helps to sharpen the conscience, ensuring that it remains sensitive to the Holy Spirit's guidance.

Additionally, prayer is a vital component of strengthening the mind. Philippians 4:6-7 instructs, "Do not be anxious about anything, but in everything by prayer and supplication with thanksgiving let your requests be made known to God. And the peace of God, which surpasses all understanding, will guard your hearts and your minds in Christ Jesus." Prayer not only brings peace but also fortifies the mind against the attacks of the enemy, enabling believers to stand firm in their convictions.

What It Means to Be Sound in Mind

Being "sound in mind" is a concept that the Bible emphasizes as crucial for spiritual health and maturity. To be sound in mind means to have a mind that is disciplined, clear, and focused on the truths of God's Word. It involves thinking soberly, being self-controlled, and having a balanced perspective that is not easily swayed by emotions or external pressures.

1 Peter 4:7 urges believers to be sound in mind: "But the end of all things is at hand: be ye therefore sober, and watch unto prayer." Here, Peter links soundness of mind with the ability to remain vigilant and prayerful, especially in light of the imminent return of Christ. A sound mind is not one that is detached from reality or indifferent to the world's challenges, but rather one that is grounded in truth and capable of discerning the times.

The Apostle Paul also highlights the importance of soundness of mind in 2 Timothy 1:7, where he writes, "For God has not given us a spirit of fear, but of power and of love and of a sound mind." This verse indicates that a sound mind is a gift from God, one that counteracts fear and enables believers to live with power and love. It is a mind that is governed by God's Spirit, not by fear or anxiety.

To be sound in mind means to exercise self-control, especially in the face of temptation. Titus 2:11-12 teaches, "For the grace of God has appeared that offers salvation to all people. It teaches us to say 'No' to ungodliness and worldly passions, and to live self-controlled, upright and godly lives in this present age." A sound mind is essential for living in accordance with God's will, rejecting the fleeting pleasures of sin, and embracing a life of holiness.

How to Be Sound in Mind

Achieving soundness of mind is not an automatic process but requires deliberate effort and reliance on God's grace. The following steps, grounded in Scripture, provide a pathway to cultivating a sound mind.

First, it is crucial to renew the mind through the Word of God. Romans 12:2 instructs, "Do not be conformed to this world, but be transformed by the renewal of your mind, that by testing you may discern what is the will of God, what is good and acceptable and perfect." The renewal of the mind is a transformative process that involves rejecting worldly patterns of thinking and embracing the truths of Scripture. This renewal is not a one-time event but a continual process of aligning one's thoughts with God's Word.

Second, practicing self-discipline is key to maintaining a sound mind. Proverbs 25:28 warns, "A man without self-control is like a city broken into and left without walls." Without self-discipline, the mind becomes vulnerable to negative influences and destructive habits. Discipline involves setting boundaries for what one allows into the mind, whether through media consumption, conversations, or other influences. It also means being intentional about cultivating positive habits, such as regular prayer, Bible study, and fellowship with other believers.

Third, cultivating a spirit of humility is essential for soundness of mind. Philippians 2:3-4 advises, "Do nothing from selfish ambition or conceit, but in humility count others more significant than yourselves. Let each of you look not only to his own interests but also to the interests of others." Humility keeps the mind from becoming prideful or self-centered, allowing it to remain open to God's guidance and correction.

Fourth, guarding the mind against anxiety and fear is necessary for soundness of mind. Isaiah 26:3 promises, "You keep him in perfect peace whose mind is stayed on you, because he trusts in you." Trusting in God and keeping the mind focused on Him brings peace, which is vital for maintaining mental stability and soundness.

Finally, staying vigilant and alert is a critical component of soundness of mind. 1 Peter 5:8 warns, "Be sober-minded; be watchful. Your adversary the devil prowls around like a roaring lion, seeking someone to devour." A sound mind is one that remains watchful, aware of the spiritual dangers that exist, and prepared to resist them through faith and obedience.

Why It Is Urgent to Be Sound in Mind

The urgency of being sound in mind is underscored by the times in which we live. The Bible repeatedly emphasizes the importance of being prepared and alert, especially as the return of Christ draws near.

Matthew 24:42-44 records Jesus' admonition to His disciples: "Therefore, stay awake, for you do not know on what day your Lord is coming. But know this, that if the master of the house had known in what part of the night the thief was coming, he would have stayed awake and would not have let his house be broken into. Therefore you also must be ready, for the Son of Man is coming at an hour you do not expect."

This sense of urgency is echoed in 1 Thessalonians 5:6-8, where Paul exhorts believers, "So then let us not sleep, as others do, but let us keep awake and be sober. For those who sleep, sleep at night, and those who get drunk, are drunk at night. But since we belong to the day, let us be sober, having put on the breastplate of faith and love, and for a helmet the hope of salvation." The metaphor of staying awake and sober points to the necessity of having a sound mind, one that is not lulled into complacency by the distractions and deceptions of the world.

In these last days, the spiritual battle for the mind is intensifying, making it all the more urgent for believers to be sound in mind. 2 Timothy 3:1-5 describes the perilous times that will characterize the last days, marked by rampant sin and rebellion against God. Paul warns, "But understand this, that in the last days there will come times of difficulty. For people will be lovers of self, lovers of money, proud, arrogant, abusive, disobedient to their parents, ungrateful, unholy, heartless, unappeasable, slanderous, without self-control, brutal, not loving good, treacherous, reckless, swollen with conceit, lovers of pleasure rather than lovers of God, having the appearance of godliness, but denying its power. Avoid such people."

This passage underscores the urgency of cultivating a sound mind, as the influences of the world become increasingly corrupt. To remain steadfast in the faith, believers must be diligent in guarding their minds and adhering to the truths of Scripture.

How Soundness of Mind Safeguards Us

Soundness of mind is not only essential for spiritual growth but also serves as a safeguard against the deceptions and temptations of the enemy. A mind that is grounded in truth and disciplined in thought is less susceptible to the lies and schemes of Satan. Ephesians 4:14 warns against spiritual immaturity, stating, "so that we may no longer be children, tossed to and fro by the waves and carried about by every wind of doctrine, by human cunning, by craftiness in deceitful schemes."

A sound mind, therefore, acts as a stabilizing force, enabling believers to discern truth from error and to stand firm in their convictions. This discernment is especially important in a world where false teachings and ideologies are prevalent. 2 Corinthians 10:5 instructs, "We destroy arguments and every lofty opinion raised against the knowledge of God, and take every thought captive to obey Christ." By taking thoughts captive and subjecting them to the truth of Scripture, believers protect themselves from being led astray.

In addition to safeguarding against deception, soundness of mind also protects against the emotional and psychological assaults that can arise from living in a fallen world. Isaiah 41:10 offers comfort and assurance, "Fear not, for I am with you; be not dismayed, for I am your God; I will strengthen you, I will help you, I will uphold you with my righteous right hand." A sound mind is anchored in the promises of God, providing stability and peace even in the midst of trials.

Furthermore, soundness of mind enables believers to navigate relationships with wisdom and grace. James 3:17 describes the qualities of heavenly wisdom: "But the wisdom from above is first pure, then peaceable, gentle, open to reason, full of mercy and good fruits, impartial and sincere." A sound mind, informed by godly wisdom, fosters healthy and edifying interactions with others, promoting unity and love within the body of Christ.

No Longer Walk in the Futility of the Old Mind

The call to put off the old person and put on the new includes a decisive break from the futile thinking that characterized our former way of life. Ephesians 4:17-18 exhorts, "Now this I say and testify in the Lord, that you must no longer walk as the Gentiles do, in the futility of their minds. They are darkened in their understanding, alienated from the life of God because of the ignorance that is in them, due to their hardness of heart."

The "futility" of the old mind refers to the emptiness and meaninglessness that results from living apart from God. Before coming to faith in Christ, our minds were dominated by worldly values and desires, leading to spiritual blindness and separation from God. Romans 1:21 describes this condition: "For although they knew God, they did not honor him as God or give thanks to him, but they became futile in their thinking, and their foolish hearts were darkened."

As believers, we are called to reject this futile mindset and embrace the renewed mind that comes through Christ. Colossians 3:2 instructs, "Set your minds on things that are above, not on things that are on earth." This shift in focus is essential for living a life that is pleasing to God and free from the bondage of sin.

The process of putting off the old mind involves a conscious effort to identify and discard thoughts and beliefs that are contrary to Scripture. 2 Corinthians 5:17 declares, "Therefore, if anyone is in Christ, he is a new creation. The old has passed away; behold, the new has come." This transformation is both an immediate reality and an ongoing process, as we continually renew our minds and conform to the image of Christ.

Prepare Your Mind for Action

Having a sound mind is not merely an end in itself but is meant to equip us for action. 1 Peter 1:13 exhorts, "Therefore, preparing your minds for action, and being sober-minded, set your hope fully on the grace that will be brought to you at the revelation of Jesus Christ." This verse highlights the active nature of the Christian life, where soundness of mind serves as the foundation for effective service and obedience to God.

Preparing the mind for action involves several key practices. First, it requires a clear understanding of God's will as revealed in Scripture. Psalm 119:105 declares, "Your word is a lamp to my feet and a light to my path." By studying and meditating on the Word of God, we gain the wisdom and discernment needed to navigate life's challenges and make decisions that honor God.

Second, it involves a readiness to respond to the promptings of the Holy Spirit. While there is no indwelling of the Holy Spirit in the believer, as the Spirit-inspired Word of God guides us, we must be sensitive to its direction. Romans 8:14 states, "For all who are led by the Spirit of God are sons of God." Being led by the Spirit through the Word requires a heart that is attuned to God's voice and a mind that is willing to obey.

Third, preparing the mind for action requires vigilance and alertness. 1 Thessalonians 5:6 reminds us, "So then let us not sleep, as others do, but let us keep awake and be sober." The Christian life is one of constant readiness, where we must be prepared to act in accordance with God's will at a moment's notice.

Finally, it involves perseverance in the face of opposition and adversity. Hebrews 12:1 encourages, "Therefore, since we are surrounded by so great a cloud of witnesses, let us also lay aside every weight, and sin which clings so closely, and let us run with endurance the race that is set before us." A sound mind is essential for maintaining the endurance needed to finish the race of faith.

Winning the Battle for Your Mind

Winning the battle for the mind is a lifelong process that requires ongoing commitment and reliance on God's grace. It involves recognizing the spiritual nature of the battle, cultivating a sound mind, and taking deliberate steps to guard and renew the mind.

Victory in this battle is not achieved through human effort alone but through the power of God working in and through us. Philippians 2:12-13 emphasizes the partnership between God's work and our responsibility: "Therefore, my beloved, as you have always obeyed, so now, not only as in my presence but much more in my absence, work out your own salvation with fear and trembling, for it is God who works in you, both to will and to work for his good pleasure." This passage highlights the importance of our active participation in the process of sanctification, while also recognizing that it is ultimately God who empowers us to live according to His will.

To win the battle for the mind, we must be diligent in filling our minds with the truth of Scripture. Colossians 3:16 exhorts, "Let the word of Christ dwell in you richly, teaching and admonishing one another in all wisdom, singing psalms and hymns and spiritual songs, with thankfulness in your hearts to God." By immersing ourselves in God's Word, we fortify our minds against the lies of the enemy and equip ourselves for spiritual warfare.

Additionally, we must be committed to prayer, recognizing that it is through prayer that we access the strength and wisdom of God. James 1:5 encourages, "If any of you lacks wisdom, let him ask God, who gives generously to all without reproach, and it will be given him." Prayer is a vital weapon in the battle for the mind, enabling us to seek God's guidance and protection.

Finally, we must be vigilant in guarding our minds against negative influences and distractions. Proverbs 4:23 advises, "Keep your heart with all vigilance, for from it flow the springs of life." This involves being selective about what we allow into our minds, whether through media, conversations, or other sources. By guarding our minds, we protect ourselves from the infiltration of worldly values and ensure that our thoughts remain aligned with God's truth.

Maintaining Your New Mind – the Mind of Christ

Once we have begun to win the battle for the mind, it is crucial to maintain the progress we have made. The Bible calls us to continually renew our minds and conform to the image of Christ. Philippians 2:5 urges, "Have this mind among yourselves, which is yours in Christ Jesus." The mind of Christ is characterized by humility, obedience, and a focus on God's will above all else.

Maintaining the mind of Christ involves a daily commitment to living according to His example. This includes practicing humility, as seen in Philippians 2:6-8, "who, though he was in the form of God, did not count equality with God a thing to be grasped, but emptied

PUT OFF THE OLD PERSON

himself, by taking the form of a servant, being born in the likeness of men. And being found in human form, he humbled himself by becoming obedient to the point of death, even death on a cross."

It also involves a focus on obedience to God's will, as demonstrated by Jesus' submission to the Father's plan. John 4:34 records Jesus' words, "My food is to do the will of him who sent me and to accomplish his work." This mindset of obedience should guide our thoughts and actions, leading us to prioritize God's purposes over our own desires.

Furthermore, maintaining the mind of Christ requires ongoing renewal through Scripture and prayer. Romans 12:2 once again emphasizes the importance of this renewal: "Do not be conformed to this world, but be transformed by the renewal of your mind, that by testing you may discern what is the will of God, what is good and acceptable and perfect." By continually immersing ourselves in God's Word and seeking His guidance, we ensure that our minds remain aligned with His will.

Finally, maintaining the mind of Christ involves being vigilant against the subtle influences that can lead us astray. 2 Corinthians 11:3 warns, "But I am afraid that as the serpent deceived Eve by his cunning, your thoughts will be led astray from a sincere and pure devotion to Christ." This vigilance requires us to be discerning and to actively resist any thoughts or ideas that contradict the truth of Scripture.

In conclusion, winning and maintaining the battle for the mind is essential for putting off the old person and putting on the new. It involves a commitment to cultivating a sound mind, grounded in Scripture, and guided by the Holy Spirit. By taking every thought captive to the obedience of Christ and continually renewing our minds, we can experience the transformation that leads to a life that glorifies God.

CHAPTER 3 How Can We Be Biblically Minded?

Have the Same Mental Attitude that Christ Jesus Had

To be biblically minded means to align our thoughts, attitudes, and actions with the teachings and example of Jesus Christ as revealed in Scripture. The Bible provides us with a clear model of the mindset we are to cultivate: "Have this mind among yourselves, which is yours in Christ Jesus" (Philippians 2:5). This command is not merely about thinking positively or adopting a religious mindset; it calls for a radical transformation of the way we perceive, interpret, and respond to the world around us, following the example set by Jesus himself.

Jesus' mental attitude was characterized by humility, obedience, and a complete submission to the will of Jehovah. Philippians 2:6-8 describes this mindset in detail: "Though he was in the form of God, he did not count equality with God a thing to be grasped, but emptied himself, by taking the form of a servant, being born in the likeness of men. And being found in human form, he humbled himself by becoming obedient to the point of death, even death on a cross." This passage reveals the profound humility of Jesus, who, despite his divine nature, chose to humble himself and obey the Father's will, even to the point of suffering and death.

Having the same mental attitude as Christ involves more than just imitating his actions; it requires a deep internal change that reorients our priorities and values to align with God's will. Romans 12:2 instructs, "Do not be conformed to this world, but be transformed by the renewal of your mind, that by testing you may discern what is the will of God, what is good and acceptable and perfect." The renewal of the mind is a continuous process of rejecting worldly influences and embracing the teachings of Scripture, allowing God's Word to shape our thoughts and attitudes.

To cultivate this Christlike mindset, it is essential to immerse ourselves in the study of Scripture, allowing it to saturate our minds and influence our daily decisions. Colossians 3:16 encourages, "Let the word of Christ dwell in you richly, teaching and admonishing one another in all wisdom, singing psalms and hymns and spiritual songs, with thankfulness in your hearts to God." As we allow the Word of God to dwell in us, it transforms our thinking, enabling us to respond to life's challenges with the same humility, obedience, and love that characterized Jesus.

Making God's Thoughts Your Own

Being biblically minded means adopting God's thoughts as our own, allowing his wisdom to guide our decisions and actions. This process begins with a commitment to understanding God's will as revealed in Scripture. Isaiah 55:8-9 reminds us, "For my thoughts are not your thoughts, neither are your ways my ways, declares Jehovah. For as the heavens are higher than the earth, so are my ways higher than your ways and my thoughts than your thoughts." This passage highlights the vast difference between human wisdom and God's perfect understanding, emphasizing the need for us to seek his guidance in all things.

To make God's thoughts our own, we must first recognize the limitations of our human understanding and be willing to submit to the authority of Scripture. Proverbs 3:5-6 instructs, "Trust in Jehovah with all your heart, and do not lean on your own understanding. In all your ways acknowledge him, and he will make straight your paths." Trusting in God's wisdom requires us to let go of our preconceived notions and embrace the truth of his Word, even when it challenges our natural inclinations.

The process of adopting God's thoughts involves a deliberate and ongoing engagement with Scripture. Psalm 1:2-3 describes the blessed man as one whose "delight is in the law of Jehovah, and on his law he meditates day and night. He is like a tree planted by streams of water that yields its fruit in its season, and its leaf does not wither. In all that he does, he prospers." This passage emphasizes the importance of meditating on God's Word, allowing it to take root in our hearts and produce spiritual fruit in our lives.

As we meditate on Scripture, we begin to internalize God's thoughts, which then influence our actions and decisions. Psalm 119:105 declares, "Your word is a lamp to my feet and a light to my path." The Word of God provides the guidance we need to navigate the complexities of life, illuminating the path of righteousness and helping us avoid the pitfalls of sin.

In addition to studying Scripture, prayer is a vital component of making God's thoughts our own. Through prayer, we invite God's wisdom into our hearts and minds, asking him to align our thoughts with his. James 1:5 encourages, "If any of you lacks wisdom, let him ask God, who gives generously to all without reproach, and it will be given him." By seeking God's wisdom in prayer, we open ourselves to the transformative work of the Holy Spirit, who guides us into all truth and helps us conform our thoughts to God's will.

Being Biblically Minded

To be biblically minded is to have a worldview that is shaped and governed by the teachings of Scripture. It involves viewing every aspect of life—our relationships, decisions, challenges, and goals—through the lens of God's Word. This biblical perspective provides the foundation for a life that is pleasing to God and effective in fulfilling his purposes.

The importance of being biblically minded is emphasized throughout Scripture. In Deuteronomy 6:6-7, Jehovah commands the Israelites, "And these words that I command you today shall be on your heart. You shall teach them diligently to your children, and shall talk of them when you sit in your house, and when you walk by the way, and when you lie down, and when you rise." This instruction highlights the centrality of God's Word in the daily life of the believer, emphasizing the need for constant engagement with Scripture in order to cultivate a biblically minded outlook.

Being biblically minded also means allowing God's Word to influence our speech and conduct. Colossians 4:6 advises, "Let your speech always be gracious, seasoned with salt, so that you may know how you ought to answer each person." Our words and actions should reflect the principles of Scripture, demonstrating the wisdom and grace that come from a mind shaped by God's truth.

Furthermore, being biblically minded equips us to resist the temptations and deceptions of the world. Ephesians 6:11-13 exhorts, "Put on the whole armor of God, that you may be able to stand against the schemes of the devil. For we do not wrestle against flesh and blood, but against the rulers, against the authorities, against the cosmic powers over this present darkness, against the spiritual forces of evil in the heavenly places. Therefore take up the whole armor of God, that you may be able to withstand in the evil day, and having done all, to stand firm." The armor of God, which includes the "sword of the Spirit, which is the word of God" (Ephesians 6:17), provides the protection and strength we need to stand firm in our faith and resist the influence of the world.

Biblically Minded and the Fruitage of the Spirit

A biblically minded person will naturally exhibit the fruitage of the Spirit, as described in Galatians 5:22-23: "But the fruit of the Spirit is love, joy, peace, patience, kindness, goodness, faithfulness, gentleness, self-control; against such things there is no law." These qualities are the outward expression of a mind that is aligned with God's Word and guided by his Spirit.

The fruitage of the Spirit is not something that can be manufactured through human effort; it is the result of a life that is surrendered to God's will and continually nourished by his Word. John 15:4-5 records Jesus' teaching on this principle: "Abide in me, and I in you. As the branch cannot bear fruit by itself, unless it abides in the vine, neither can you, unless you abide in me. I am the vine; you are the branches. Whoever abides in me and I in him, he it is that bears much fruit, for apart from me you can do nothing."

Being biblically minded means remaining in close fellowship with Christ, allowing his Word to shape our thoughts, attitudes, and actions.

As we abide in Christ and his Word abides in us, the fruit of the Spirit will naturally manifest in our lives, demonstrating the transformative power of God's truth.

The fruitage of the Spirit serves as evidence of spiritual maturity and a life that is pleasing to God. Matthew 7:16-20 emphasizes the importance of bearing good fruit: "You will recognize them by their fruits. Are grapes gathered from thornbushes, or figs from thistles? So, every healthy tree bears good fruit, but the diseased tree bears bad fruit. A healthy tree cannot bear bad fruit, nor can a diseased tree bear good fruit. Every tree that does not bear good fruit is cut down and thrown into the fire. Thus you will recognize them by their fruits." The fruit we produce is a reflection of the condition of our hearts and the influence of God's Word in our lives.

How Are Bible Study and Meditation Related to Making God's Thoughts Our Own?

Bible study and meditation are essential practices for making God's thoughts our own. Through diligent study of Scripture, we gain a deeper understanding of God's character, his will, and his purposes. 2 Timothy 3:16-17 declares, "All Scripture is breathed out by God and profitable for teaching, for reproof, for correction, and for training in righteousness, that the man of God may be complete, equipped for every good work." The study of God's Word equips us with the knowledge and wisdom needed to live a life that is aligned with his will.

Meditation, on the other hand, involves taking the truths of Scripture and pondering them deeply, allowing them to penetrate our hearts and minds. Psalm 119:97 expresses the value of meditation: "Oh how I love your law! It is my meditation all the day." Meditation helps to internalize God's Word, making it a part of our thought processes and influencing our decisions and actions.

The relationship between Bible study and meditation is one of mutual reinforcement. Study provides the foundation of knowledge, while meditation deepens our understanding and application of that knowledge. Joshua 1:8 emphasizes this connection: "This Book of the

Law shall not depart from your mouth, but you shall meditate on it day and night, so that you may be careful to do according to all that is written in it. For then you will make your way prosperous, and then you will have good success." By meditating on God's Word, we ensure that it remains at the forefront of our minds, guiding our thoughts and actions in every situation.

Furthermore, meditation on Scripture helps us to develop a biblical mindset, where God's thoughts become our own. Psalm 1:2-3 again illustrates the transformative power of meditation: "but his delight is in the law of Jehovah, and on his law he meditates day and night. He is like a tree planted by streams of water that yields its fruit in its season, and its leaf does not wither. In all that he does, he prospers." As we meditate on God's Word, we are continually nourished by his truth, enabling us to grow in spiritual maturity and bear fruit for his glory.

God's Thinking Should Have What Effect on Our Actions?

The thoughts of God, as revealed in Scripture, should have a profound and transformative effect on our actions. James 1:22 exhorts, "But be doers of the word, and not hearers only, deceiving yourselves." This verse emphasizes the importance of translating the knowledge of God's Word into practical, obedient action. It is not enough to simply understand God's thoughts; we must allow them to shape our behavior and decisions.

The effect of God's thinking on our actions is seen in the way we live out our faith in everyday life. Colossians 3:12-14 provides a practical example of how God's thoughts should influence our behavior: "Put on then, as God's chosen ones, holy and beloved, compassionate hearts, kindness, humility, meekness, and patience, bearing with one another and, if one has a complaint against another, forgiving each other; as the Lord has forgiven you, so you also must forgive. And above all these put on love, which binds everything together in perfect harmony." These qualities are a direct reflection of God's character and his expectations for how we are to treat others.

Furthermore, God's thoughts should lead us to pursue righteousness and holiness in all areas of life. 1 Peter 1:15-16 instructs, "but as he who called you is holy, you also be holy in all your conduct, since it is written, 'You shall be holy, for I am holy.'" The call to holiness is a call to align our actions with the character of God, rejecting sinful behavior and striving to live in a way that honors him.

God's thinking also affects our actions by guiding our decisions and priorities. Proverbs 16:3 advises, "Commit your work to Jehovah, and your plans will be established." When we align our thoughts with God's will, our actions naturally follow, leading to decisions that are pleasing to him and in line with his purposes.

Finally, the effect of God's thinking on our actions is seen in our commitment to sharing the Gospel and making disciples. Matthew 28:19-20 records Jesus' Great Commission: "Go therefore and make disciples of all nations, baptizing them in the name of the Father and of the Son and of the Holy Spirit, teaching them to observe all that I have commanded you. And behold, I am with you always, to the end of the age." As we adopt God's thoughts as our own, we are compelled to share his truth with others and to live out the mission he has given us.

How Can Meditating on God's Thoughts Help Us with Future Decisions?

Meditating on God's thoughts equips us with the wisdom and discernment needed to make sound decisions in the future. Psalm 119:11 declares, "I have stored up your word in my heart, that I might not sin against you." By internalizing God's Word through meditation, we prepare ourselves to face future challenges and make decisions that align with his will.

Meditation on Scripture helps to develop a deep understanding of God's character and his principles, which serve as a guide for making decisions. Proverbs 3:5-6 encourages, "Trust in Jehovah with all your heart, and do not lean on your own understanding. In all your ways acknowledge him, and he will make straight your paths." When we meditate on God's Word, we learn to trust his wisdom above our own, leading to decisions that are rooted in his truth.

Additionally, meditation helps to cultivate a sensitivity to the leading of the Holy Spirit through the Word of God. Psalm 25:4-5 expresses the desire for divine guidance: "Make me to know your ways, O Jehovah; teach me your paths. Lead me in your truth and teach me, for you are the God of my salvation; for you I wait all the day long." As we meditate on God's thoughts, we become more attuned to his guidance, enabling us to make decisions that reflect his will.

Meditating on God's Word also helps to guard against impulsive or emotionally driven decisions. Psalm 119:105 again affirms, "Your word is a lamp to my feet and a light to my path." By meditating on Scripture, we ensure that our decisions are based on God's truth rather than on fleeting emotions or worldly influences.

Finally, meditation on God's thoughts provides the peace and confidence needed to make difficult decisions. Isaiah 26:3 promises, "You keep him in perfect peace whose mind is stayed on you, because he trusts in you." When we meditate on God's Word, we experience the peace that comes from trusting in his sovereignty, allowing us to make decisions with confidence and clarity.

How Can We Identify a Spiritual Person?

A spiritual person is someone whose life is consistently aligned with the teachings of Scripture and who exhibits the fruit of the Spirit. Galatians 5:22-23 describes the qualities that characterize a spiritual person: "But the fruit of the Spirit is love, joy, peace, patience, kindness, goodness, faithfulness, gentleness, self-control; against such things there is no law." These qualities are the outward manifestation of a life that is surrendered to God and guided by his Spirit.

A spiritual person is also someone who prioritizes their relationship with God above all else. Matthew 6:33 instructs, "But seek first the kingdom of God and his righteousness, and all these things will be added to you." A spiritual person seeks God's kingdom and righteousness in every aspect of life, making decisions that reflect their commitment to his will.

Furthermore, a spiritual person is someone who is deeply engaged with God's Word. Psalm 1:2-3 describes the blessed man as one whose "delight is in the law of Jehovah, and on his law he meditates day and night." A spiritual person values Scripture as the ultimate source of truth and wisdom, allowing it to shape their thoughts, attitudes, and actions.

A spiritual person is also characterized by humility and a willingness to serve others. Philippians 2:3-4 advises, "Do nothing from selfish ambition or conceit, but in humility count others more significant than yourselves. Let each of you look not only to his own interests but also to the interests of others." A spiritual person follows the example of Christ, demonstrating humility and selflessness in their interactions with others.

Finally, a spiritual person is someone who is committed to prayer and communion with God. Colossians 4:2 exhorts, "Continue steadfastly in prayer, being watchful in it with thanksgiving." A spiritual person recognizes the importance of maintaining a close relationship with God through prayer, seeking his guidance and strength in all things.

What Can We Learn from Exemplary Spiritual People?

Exemplary spiritual people provide valuable lessons and examples for us to follow as we seek to grow in our own faith. Hebrews 13:7 encourages, "Remember your leaders, those who spoke to you the word of God. Consider the outcome of their way of life, and imitate their faith." By observing the lives of spiritual leaders and mentors, we can learn important principles of godly living and spiritual maturity.

One lesson we can learn from exemplary spiritual people is the importance of perseverance in the face of trials. James 1:12 teaches, "Blessed is the man who remains steadfast under trial, for when he has stood the test he will receive the crown of life, which God has promised to those who love him." Exemplary spiritual people demonstrate the value of remaining faithful to God, even in difficult circumstances, trusting in his promises and relying on his strength.

Another lesson is the importance of humility and dependence on God. 1 Peter 5:6-7 advises, "Humble yourselves, therefore, under the mighty hand of God so that at the proper time he may exalt you, casting all your anxieties on him, because he cares for you." Spiritual leaders who exhibit humility and a deep reliance on God serve as powerful examples of how to live a life that is pleasing to him.

We can also learn the importance of faithfulness and integrity from exemplary spiritual people. Proverbs 20:7 states, "The righteous who walks in his integrity—blessed are his children after him!" Spiritual leaders who consistently demonstrate integrity in their actions and decisions provide a model for how to live a life that honors God and serves as a witness to others.

Furthermore, exemplary spiritual people teach us the value of devotion to God's Word. Acts 17:11 commends the Bereans for their diligence in studying Scripture: "Now these Jews were more noble than those in Thessalonica; they received the word with all eagerness, examining the Scriptures daily to see if these things were so." By following the example of those who prioritize Bible study and meditation, we can deepen our own understanding of God's Word and grow in our faith.

Finally, exemplary spiritual people demonstrate the importance of love and compassion in our interactions with others. 1 John 4:7-8 exhorts, "Beloved, let us love one another, for love is from God, and whoever loves has been born of God and knows God. Anyone who does not love does not know God, because God is love." Spiritual leaders who exhibit love and compassion toward others provide a powerful witness to the transformative power of God's love in their lives.

Why Should We Strive to Be Biblically Minded?

Striving to be biblically minded is essential for living a life that is pleasing to God and fulfilling his purposes. The Bible provides the ultimate standard of truth and righteousness, and aligning our thoughts and actions with Scripture is key to spiritual growth and maturity.

One reason to strive to be biblically minded is that it enables us to know and fulfill God's will. Romans 12:2 instructs, "Do not be conformed to this world, but be transformed by the renewal of your mind, that by testing you may discern what is the will of God, what is good and acceptable and perfect." By renewing our minds with Scripture, we gain the discernment needed to understand and carry out God's will in our lives.

Another reason is that being biblically minded protects us from the deceptions and temptations of the world. Ephesians 6:11-13 exhorts us to "put on the whole armor of God, that you may be able to stand against the schemes of the devil." The armor of God, which includes the "sword of the Spirit, which is the word of God" (Ephesians 6:17), equips us to resist the influence of the world and remain steadfast in our faith.

Being biblically minded also fosters spiritual growth and maturity. 2 Timothy 3:16-17 declares, "All Scripture is breathed out by God and profitable for teaching, for reproof, for correction, and for training in righteousness, that the man of God may be complete, equipped for every good work." By immersing ourselves in God's Word, we are equipped with the knowledge and wisdom needed to grow in our faith and fulfill God's purposes.

Furthermore, striving to be biblically minded enables us to reflect God's character and values in our daily lives. Colossians 3:12-14 instructs, "Put on then, as God's chosen ones, holy and beloved, compassionate hearts, kindness, humility, meekness, and patience, bearing with one another and, if one has a complaint against another, forgiving each other; as the Lord has forgiven you, so you also must forgive. And above all these put on love, which binds everything together in perfect harmony." By adopting a biblical mindset, we are empowered to live out these qualities and demonstrate the love and grace of God to others.

Finally, striving to be biblically minded prepares us for the challenges and opportunities of life. Psalm 119:105 affirms, "Your word is a lamp to my feet and a light to my path." By allowing Scripture to guide our thoughts and actions, we are equipped to navigate the complexities of life and make decisions that honor God.

Being Biblically Minded Leads to the Mind of Christ

The ultimate goal of being biblically minded is to develop the mind of Christ, where our thoughts, attitudes, and actions are fully aligned with his. Philippians 2:5 exhorts, "Have this mind among yourselves, which is yours in Christ Jesus." The mind of Christ is characterized by humility, obedience, and a deep commitment to doing the Father's will.

Having the mind of Christ involves a continual process of transformation, where we allow God's Word to renew our minds and shape our character. Romans 12:2 once again emphasizes the importance of this renewal: "Do not be conformed to this world, but be transformed by the renewal of your mind, that by testing you may discern what is the will of God, what is good and acceptable and perfect." As we renew our minds with Scripture, we become more like Christ in our thoughts, attitudes, and actions.

The mind of Christ is also characterized by a deep love for others and a willingness to serve. Philippians 2:3-4 instructs, "Do nothing from selfish ambition or conceit, but in humility count others more significant than yourselves. Let each of you look not only to his own interests but also to the interests of others." By adopting the mind of Christ, we develop a heart of compassion and a desire to serve others, reflecting the love of God in our interactions.

Furthermore, the mind of Christ is marked by a focus on eternal values rather than temporal concerns. Colossians 3:2-3 advises, "Set your minds on things that are above, not on things that are on earth. For you have died, and your life is hidden with Christ in God." Having the mind of Christ means prioritizing God's kingdom and purposes above the fleeting pleasures and distractions of the world.

Finally, having the mind of Christ involves a commitment to obedience and faithfulness, even in the face of suffering. Hebrews 12:2 encourages, "looking to Jesus, the founder and perfecter of our faith, who for the joy that was set before him endured the cross, despising the shame, and is seated at the right hand of the throne of God." The mind of Christ is steadfast in its commitment to doing the Father's will, regardless of the cost.

By striving to be biblically minded, we are continually transformed into the likeness of Christ, developing the mind of Christ and living a life that glorifies God and fulfills his purposes.

CHAPTER 4 How Can the Renewal of Your Mind Transform Your Life?

New in the Force Actuating Your Mind

The renewal of the mind is a central theme in the Christian life, emphasizing the transformation that takes place when we align our thoughts with the will of God. The Bible repeatedly addresses the importance of this renewal, highlighting the difference between the mind of the "soulical" or "physical" man and that of the spiritual man. Colossians 3:1-2 instructs, "If then you have been raised with Christ, seek the things that are above, where Christ is, seated at the right hand of God. Set your minds on things that are above, not on things that are on earth." This passage introduces the concept of a new force actuating the mind—a force that is rooted in spiritual priorities rather than earthly concerns.

The mind of the "soulical" man, as Paul describes in 1 Corinthians 2:14-15, is unable to comprehend the things of God: "The natural person does not accept the things of the Spirit of God, for they are folly to him, and he is not able to understand them because they are spiritually discerned." This natural mind is focused on worldly matters and is incapable of grasping the depth of spiritual truths. In contrast, the spiritual man, whose mind has been renewed by the Holy Spirit through the Word of God, discerns and understands the will of God.

Ephesians 4:23 further reinforces this idea, stating, "and to be renewed in the spirit of your minds." The renewal of the mind is not merely a change in thinking but a complete transformation of the inner being. This renewal empowers believers to live in a way that pleases God, enabling them to discern his will and make decisions that align with his purposes.

This transformation is made possible by the work of the Holy Spirit, who uses the Word of God to renew and reshape our minds. Romans 12:2 emphasizes the importance of this process: "Do not be conformed to this world, but be transformed by the renewal of your mind, that by testing you may discern what is the will of God, what is good and acceptable and perfect." The renewal of the mind is essential for spiritual growth, enabling believers to resist the influence of the world and live according to the values of God's kingdom.

The 'Law of the Mind'

The apostle Paul introduces the concept of the "law of the mind" in Romans 7:21-25, where he describes the internal struggle that believers experience: "So I find it to be a law that when I want to do right, evil lies close at hand. For I delight in the law of God, in my inner being, but I see in my members another law waging war against the law of my mind and making me captive to the law of sin that dwells in my members. Wretched man that I am! Who will deliver me from this body of death? Thanks be to God through Jesus Christ our Lord! So then, I myself serve the law of God with my mind, but with my flesh I serve the law of sin."

This passage highlights the conflict between the renewed mind that desires to obey God and the flesh that is inclined toward sin. The "law of the mind" refers to the inclination of the renewed mind to delight in God's law and seek to live according to his commands. However, this inclination is opposed by the "law of sin" that operates in the flesh, leading to a constant battle between the two.

Galatians 5:16-17 further explains this conflict: "But I say, walk by the Spirit, and you will not gratify the desires of the flesh. For the desires of the flesh are against the Spirit, and the desires of the Spirit are against the flesh, for these are opposed to each other, to keep you from doing the things you want to do." The renewed mind, guided by the Holy Spirit through the Word of God, seeks to resist the flesh and live in obedience to God's will.

Understanding the "law of the mind" is crucial for believers as it helps them recognize the internal struggle they face and rely on God's strength to overcome it. The key to victory in this battle lies in submitting to the guidance of the Holy Spirit and allowing the Word of God to continually renew and transform the mind.

Dullness or Corruptness of Mind

While the renewal of the mind is essential for spiritual growth, the Bible also warns against the dangers of dullness and corruptness of mind. 2 Corinthians 3:13-14 speaks of the Israelites whose minds were hardened: "Not like Moses, who would put a veil over his face so that the Israelites might not gaze at the outcome of what was being brought to an end. But their minds were hardened. For to this day, when they read the old covenant, that same veil remains unlifted, because only through Christ is it taken away."

This passage illustrates how a mind that is resistant to the truth of God becomes dull and unable to perceive spiritual realities. The veil that Paul refers to symbolizes the spiritual blindness that results from a hardened mind—a mind that rejects the truth and remains in darkness.

Colossians 2:18 warns against allowing the mind to become corrupted by false teachings and deceptive philosophies: "Let no one disqualify you, insisting on asceticism and worship of angels, going on in detail about visions, puffed up without reason by his sensuous mind." The mind that is corrupted by such influences loses its sensitivity to the truth and becomes susceptible to error.

Romans 1:28 describes the ultimate consequence of a corrupt mind: "And since they did not see fit to acknowledge God, God gave them up to a debased mind to do what ought not to be done." A debased mind is one that has rejected God and his truth, leading to a life of sin and moral decay.

The danger of a corrupt mind is further emphasized in Ephesians 4:17-18: "Now this I say and testify in the Lord, that you must no longer walk as the Gentiles do, in the futility of their minds. They are darkened in their understanding, alienated from the life of God because of the ignorance that is in them, due to their hardness of heart." The futility and darkness of the mind result from alienation from God, leading to a life that is void of spiritual purpose and direction.

To guard against the dullness and corruptness of mind, believers must be diligent in renewing their minds with the truth of God's Word. Philippians 4:8 provides a helpful guide for this renewal: "Finally, brothers, whatever is true, whatever is honorable, whatever is just, whatever is pure, whatever is lovely, whatever is commendable, if there is any excellence, if there is anything worthy of praise, think about these things." By focusing on these virtues, believers can maintain a mind that is pure, sensitive to God's truth, and resistant to the corrupting influences of the world.

Why Is It Not Easy to Keep the Mind Renewed and Live in Harmony with It?

Keeping the mind renewed and living in harmony with it is not easy because of the ongoing battle between the flesh and the Spirit. As Paul describes in Romans 7:22-23, the renewed mind delights in God's law, but the flesh continues to wage war against it. This internal conflict creates a tension that makes it challenging to consistently live according to the renewed mind.

One of the primary reasons it is difficult to keep the mind renewed is the influence of the world. 1 John 2:15-17 warns, "Do not love the world or the things in the world. If anyone loves the world, the love of the Father is not in him. For all that is in the world—the desires of the flesh and the desires of the eyes and pride of life—is not from the Father but is from the world. And the world is passing away along with its desires, but whoever does the will of God abides forever." The world, with its values and temptations, constantly seeks to draw the believer away from God's truth and conform their mind to its standards.

Another challenge in keeping the mind renewed is the deceitfulness of sin. Hebrews 3:13 warns, "But exhort one another every day, as long as it is called 'today,' that none of you may be hardened by the deceitfulness of sin." Sin has a way of dulling the mind and hardening the heart, making it more difficult to perceive and follow God's truth. This deceitfulness can lead to a gradual drifting away from the renewed mind and a return to the old patterns of thinking and behavior.

Additionally, spiritual warfare plays a significant role in the difficulty of keeping the mind renewed. Ephesians 6:12 reminds us, "For we do not wrestle against flesh and blood, but against the rulers, against the authorities, against the cosmic powers over this present darkness, against the spiritual forces of evil in the heavenly places." The enemy seeks to undermine the renewal of the mind by planting doubts, fears, and lies that distract and discourage the believer.

Despite these challenges, the Bible encourages believers to persevere in the renewal of the mind. Romans 12:12 offers this exhortation: "Rejoice in hope, be patient in tribulation, be constant in prayer." By maintaining hope, patience, and a consistent prayer life, believers can continue to renew their minds and live in harmony with the truth of God's Word.

Paul Describes the Battle You Have with Your Bodies

The apostle Paul provides a vivid description of the battle that believers have with their bodies in Romans 7:18-19: "For I know that nothing good dwells in me, that is, in my flesh. For I have the desire to do what is right, but not the ability to carry it out. For I do not do the good I want, but the evil I do not want is what I keep on doing." This passage captures the frustration and struggle that many believers experience as they seek to live according to the renewed mind while contending with the sinful desires of the flesh.

Paul's struggle with the flesh is not unique; it is a common experience for all believers. Galatians 5:17 explains, "For the desires of the flesh are against the Spirit, and the desires of the Spirit are against the flesh, for these are opposed to each other, to keep you from doing the things you want to do." The flesh, with its sinful inclinations, resists the work of the Holy Spirit and the renewal of the mind, creating an ongoing battle within the believer.

This battle is further described in Romans 8:5-6: "For those who live according to the flesh set their minds on the things of the flesh, but those who live according to the Spirit set their minds on the things of the Spirit. For to set the mind on the flesh is death, but to set the mind on the Spirit is life and peace." The mind that is set on the flesh leads to death, while the mind that is set on the Spirit leads to life and peace. This contrast highlights the importance of renewing the mind and setting it on the things of the Spirit in order to overcome the desires of the flesh.

Paul's solution to this battle is found in Romans 8:12-13: "So then, brothers, we are debtors, not to the flesh, to live according to the flesh. For if you live according to the flesh you will die, but if by the Spirit you put to death the deeds of the body, you will live." The key to victory in this battle is to "put to death" the deeds of the body by the power of the Holy Spirit. This involves a daily commitment to deny the flesh and live according to the renewed mind that is guided by the Spirit and grounded in the Word of God.

Upon What Must You Set Your Minds?

The Bible is clear that believers must set their minds on the things of God, rather than on earthly or fleshly concerns. Colossians 3:2 instructs, "Set your minds on things that are above, not on things that are on earth." This verse emphasizes the importance of maintaining a heavenly perspective, focusing on the eternal rather than the temporal. By setting our minds on things above, we align our thoughts with God's will and values, allowing them to guide our actions and decisions.

Romans 8:5-6 reiterates this principle: "For those who live according to the flesh set their minds on the things of the flesh, but those who live according to the Spirit set their minds on the things of the Spirit. For to set the mind on the flesh is death, but to set the mind on the Spirit is life and peace." The mind that is set on the flesh leads to spiritual death, while the mind that is set on the Spirit leads to life and peace. This contrast underscores the critical importance of setting our minds on the things of the Spirit in order to experience the fullness of life that God intends for us.

Philippians 4:8 provides further guidance on the types of things that should occupy our minds: "Finally, brothers, whatever is true, whatever is honorable, whatever is just, whatever is pure, whatever is lovely, whatever is commendable, if there is any excellence, if there is anything worthy of praise, think about these things." By focusing on these virtues, we cultivate a mind that is aligned with God's character and resistant to the corrupting influences of the world.

In addition to setting our minds on godly things, the Bible also calls us to set our minds on the mission and purpose that God has given us. Matthew 6:33 instructs, "But seek first the kingdom of God and his righteousness, and all these things will be added to you." By prioritizing God's kingdom and righteousness, we ensure that our minds are focused on the things that truly matter, allowing us to live in a way that honors God and advances his purposes.

Setting our minds on the things of God is not a passive process; it requires intentional effort and discipline. 2 Corinthians 10:5 encourages, "We destroy arguments and every lofty opinion raised against the knowledge of God, and take every thought captive to obey Christ." By taking every thought captive and making it obedient to Christ, we actively participate in the renewal of our minds, allowing God's truth to shape our thinking and guide our actions.

Remembering What Warning Example, Why Fear Corruption of Mind?

The Bible provides several warning examples that illustrate the dangers of a corrupted mind and the consequences of turning away from God's truth. One of the most significant examples is that of Eve, who, despite having a perfect mind and a natural inclination toward good, was deceived by the serpent and led into sin. Genesis 3:1-6 records the interaction between Eve and the serpent, where the serpent's deception caused Eve to doubt God's command and ultimately disobey it.

The story of Eve serves as a powerful warning about the ease with which the mind can be corrupted, even when it is naturally inclined toward good. 2 Corinthians 11:3 references this example, saying, "But

I am afraid that as the serpent deceived Eve by his cunning, your thoughts will be led astray from a sincere and pure devotion to Christ." Paul's concern is that believers might be similarly deceived and led away from their devotion to Christ, emphasizing the need for vigilance in guarding the mind against corruption.

The fear of corruption of the mind is further justified by the warnings given in Scripture about the consequences of turning away from God's truth. Romans 1:28 describes the tragic outcome of a mind that has rejected God: "And since they did not see fit to acknowledge God, God gave them up to a debased mind to do what ought not to be done." A debased mind, corrupted by sin, leads to moral decay and a life that is contrary to God's will.

This fear of corruption is also reflected in the teachings of Jesus, who warned against the dangers of a divided mind. In Matthew 6:22-23, Jesus said, "The eye is the lamp of the body. So, if your eye is healthy, your whole body will be full of light, but if your eye is bad, your whole body will be full of darkness. If then the light in you is darkness, how great is the darkness!" The "eye" in this context represents the focus and intention of the mind; if the mind is corrupted or divided, it leads to spiritual darkness and confusion.

To prevent the corruption of the mind, believers must be diligent in renewing their minds with the truth of God's Word and remaining vigilant against the subtle deceptions of the enemy. Ephesians 4:22-24 encourages, "to put off your old self, which belongs to your former manner of life and is corrupt through deceitful desires, and to be renewed in the spirit of your minds, and to put on the new self, created after the likeness of God in true righteousness and holiness." By continually renewing our minds and embracing the new self in Christ, we guard against the corruption that can lead us away from God's truth.

Where Does Enmity Against God Start?

Enmity against God begins in the mind, where sinful thoughts and attitudes take root and grow into rebellion against God's will. Romans 8:7 explains, "For the mind that is set on the flesh is hostile

PUT OFF THE OLD PERSON

to God, for it does not submit to God's law; indeed, it cannot." A mind that is focused on the desires of the flesh becomes hostile to God, rejecting his authority and resisting his commands. This hostility, or enmity, is not merely a passive indifference but an active opposition to God's truth.

The origin of enmity against God is further illustrated in James 4:4, which warns, "You adulterous people! Do you not know that friendship with the world is enmity with God? Therefore whoever wishes to be a friend of the world makes himself an enemy of God." When the mind is set on the values and priorities of the world, it naturally becomes opposed to the values and priorities of God, leading to enmity with him.

This enmity is not limited to those who are openly rebellious against God; it can also exist in those who profess faith but allow their minds to be influenced by worldly desires. Matthew 6:24 emphasizes the impossibility of serving two masters: "No one can serve two masters, for either he will hate the one and love the other, or he will be devoted to the one and despise the other. You cannot serve God and money." A divided mind, one that seeks to serve both God and worldly interests, ultimately becomes an enemy of God, as it cannot fully submit to his will.

The danger of enmity against God is also highlighted in Colossians 1:21, which describes the condition of those who are alienated from God: "And you, who once were alienated and hostile in mind, doing evil deeds." The hostility of the mind leads to evil actions, further entrenching the individual in opposition to God. This alienation from God is the result of a mind that has rejected his truth and embraced sin.

To combat the enmity that starts in the mind, believers must actively seek to renew their minds and align their thoughts with God's will. Romans 12:2 again provides the key to overcoming this enmity: "Do not be conformed to this world, but be transformed by the renewal of your mind, that by testing you may discern what is the will of God, what is good and acceptable and perfect." By allowing the Holy Spirit to renew and transform our minds, we can overcome the enmity that arises from sinful thoughts and live in harmony with God's truth.

We Cannot Wholeheartedly Serve God with a Double Mind

The Bible is clear that serving God with a double mind—one that is divided between God and worldly desires—is impossible. Psalm 119:113 expresses this sentiment: "I hate the double-minded, but I love your law." A double mind is one that is unstable and indecisive, lacking the full commitment to follow God's will. This instability prevents the individual from wholeheartedly serving God and living according to his truth.

Jesus addresses the issue of a double mind in Revelation 3:16, where he rebukes the church in Laodicea: "So, because you are lukewarm, and neither hot nor cold, I will spit you out of my mouth." The lukewarmness of the Laodiceans reflects a divided allegiance, where they were neither fully committed to God nor fully opposed to him. This half-hearted devotion is unacceptable to God, as it demonstrates a lack of true commitment and sincerity.

James 1:8 also warns of the dangers of a double mind: "he is a double-minded man, unstable in all his ways." A double-minded person is characterized by instability and inconsistency, unable to fully trust in God or follow his commands. This lack of stability hinders spiritual growth and prevents the individual from experiencing the fullness of life that God offers.

The call to wholehearted devotion is echoed in Matthew 22:37, where Jesus teaches, "And he said to him, 'You shall love the Lord your God with all your heart and with all your soul and with all your mind.'" This command requires a complete and undivided commitment to God, where every aspect of the individual's being—heart, soul, and mind—is fully devoted to loving and serving him.

To overcome the double mind and serve God wholeheartedly, believers must actively renew their minds and set their focus on God's truth. Philippians 3:13-14 provides a helpful perspective: "Brothers, I do not consider that I have made it my own. But one thing I do:

forgetting what lies behind and straining forward to what lies ahead, I press on toward the goal for the prize of the upward call of God in Christ Jesus." By focusing on the goal of following Christ and pressing forward in faith, believers can overcome the double mind and live a life that is fully committed to serving God.

How and Why Must You Brace Up Your Minds to Survive This Wicked Age?

The Bible frequently warns believers about the dangers of living in a wicked age and the need to brace up their minds in order to survive spiritually. 1 Peter 1:13 exhorts, "Therefore, preparing your minds for action, and being sober-minded, set your hope fully on the grace that will be brought to you at the revelation of Jesus Christ." This verse emphasizes the importance of mental preparation and sobriety in the face of the challenges posed by a sinful world. Bracing up the mind involves being alert, disciplined, and focused on the hope of Christ's return.

The necessity of bracing up the mind is further underscored by the pervasive influence of evil in the world. 2 Timothy 3:1-5 describes the characteristics of the last days: "But understand this, that in the last days there will come times of difficulty. For people will be lovers of self, lovers of money, proud, arrogant, abusive, disobedient to their parents, ungrateful, unholy, heartless, unappeasable, slanderous, without self-control, brutal, not loving good, treacherous, reckless, swollen with conceit, lovers of pleasure rather than lovers of God, having the appearance of godliness, but denying its power. Avoid such people." In such a wicked age, the mind must be braced and fortified against the temptations and deceptions that abound.

Bracing up the mind also involves standing firm in the face of persecution and opposition. Ephesians 6:13 advises, "Therefore take up the whole armor of God, that you may be able to withstand in the evil day, and having done all, to stand firm." The armor of God, which includes the helmet of salvation and the sword of the Spirit (the Word of God), equips believers to withstand the attacks of the enemy and remain steadfast in their faith.

The reason for bracing up the mind is not only for personal spiritual survival but also for the sake of being a witness to others. Matthew 5:14-16 encourages believers to be a light in the darkness: "You are the light of the world. A city set on a hill cannot be hidden. Nor do people light a lamp and put it under a basket, but on a stand, and it gives light to all in the house. In the same way, let your light shine before others, so that they may see your good works and give glory to your Father who is in heaven." By bracing up their minds and living according to God's truth, believers can shine as lights in a wicked world, pointing others to the hope and salvation found in Christ.

To brace up the mind effectively, believers must remain rooted in the Word of God and vigilant in prayer. Colossians 4:2 encourages, "Continue steadfastly in prayer, being watchful in it with thanksgiving." Prayer and watchfulness are essential components of bracing up the mind, enabling believers to stay alert and prepared for the challenges of living in a wicked age.

Be Transformed by Making Your Mind Over

The transformation of the believer's life begins with the renewal of the mind. Romans 12:2 again emphasizes this transformative process: "Do not be conformed to this world, but be transformed by the renewal of your mind, that by testing you may discern what is the will of God, what is good and acceptable and perfect." The command to "make your mind over" involves a deliberate and ongoing process of rejecting the patterns of the world and embracing the truths of Scripture.

This transformation is not superficial but deeply rooted in a change of thinking that affects every aspect of life. Ephesians 4:22-24 describes the process: "to put off your old self, which belongs to your former manner of life and is corrupt through deceitful desires, and to be renewed in the spirit of your minds, and to put on the new self, created after the likeness of God in true righteousness and holiness." The renewal of the mind leads to the putting off of the old self and the putting on of the new self, resulting in a life that reflects the character of God.

The transformation of the mind also involves a shift in focus from the temporal to the eternal. 2 Corinthians 4:18 encourages, "as we look not to the things that are seen but to the things that are unseen. For the things that are seen are transient, but the things that are unseen are eternal." By making our minds over and focusing on the eternal truths of God's Word, we are able to live with purpose and direction, regardless of the challenges we face in the present world.

The process of making the mind over is not a one-time event but a lifelong journey of growth and maturity. Philippians 3:12-14 again reflects this ongoing pursuit: "Not that I have already obtained this or am already perfect, but I press on to make it my own, because Christ Jesus has made me his own. Brothers, I do not consider that I have made it my own. But one thing I do: forgetting what lies behind and straining forward to what lies ahead, I press on toward the goal for the prize of the upward call of God in Christ Jesus." The transformation of the mind requires perseverance, as we continually press forward in our walk with Christ, allowing his Word to shape and renew our thinking.

To be transformed by the renewal of the mind, believers must commit to daily engagement with Scripture, prayer, and fellowship with other believers. By immersing themselves in the truths of God's Word and relying on the guidance of the Holy Spirit, they can experience the transformation that leads to a life of righteousness and holiness.

God's Word is Alive

The power of the renewal of the mind lies in the fact that God's Word is alive and active. Hebrews 4:12 declares, "For the word of God is living and active, sharper than any two-edged sword, piercing to the division of soul and of spirit, of joints and of marrow, and discerning the thoughts and intentions of the heart." The Word of God is not merely a collection of ancient writings; it is a living force that penetrates the depths of the human heart and mind, bringing transformation and renewal.

The living nature of God's Word is also reflected in its ability to bring about change in the believer's life. Isaiah 55:10-11 assures us of the effectiveness of God's Word: "For as the rain and the snow come down from heaven and do not return there but water the earth, making it bring forth and sprout, giving seed to the sower and bread to the eater, so shall my word be that goes out from my mouth; it shall not return to me empty, but it shall accomplish that which I purpose, and shall succeed in the thing for which I sent it." God's Word accomplishes his purposes in the lives of those who receive and apply it, bringing about the renewal and transformation that he desires.

The renewal of the mind, therefore, is not something that believers achieve on their own; it is the result of the living and active Word of God at work within them. As believers engage with Scripture, they experience its power to transform their thinking, align their desires with God's will, and guide them in living a life that honors him.

The living nature of God's Word also means that it is relevant and applicable to every aspect of life. 2 Timothy 3:16-17 again emphasizes the usefulness of Scripture: "All Scripture is breathed out by God and profitable for teaching, for reproof, for correction, and for training in righteousness, that the man of God may be complete, equipped for every good work." The renewal of the mind involves allowing God's Word to teach, correct, and train us, equipping us to live according to his purposes.

To experience the full power of God's Word in the renewal of the mind, believers must approach it with humility, reverence, and a willingness to be transformed. James 1:21 advises, "Therefore put away all filthiness and rampant wickedness and receive with meekness the implanted word, which is able to save your souls." By receiving the Word with meekness and allowing it to take root in our hearts and minds, we open ourselves to the transformative work of God in our lives.

CHAPTER 5 How Can We Keep the Mind Renewed?

What Does It Mean to Be a Spiritual Person?

To keep the mind renewed, it is essential first to understand what it means to be a spiritual person. In the biblical sense, a spiritual person is someone whose life is governed by the Holy Spirit through the Word of God rather than by the desires of the flesh. Romans 8:5-6 explains, "For those who live according to the flesh set their minds on the things of the flesh, but those who live according to the Spirit set their minds on the things of the Spirit. For to set the mind on the flesh is death, but to set the mind on the Spirit is life and peace." A spiritual person, therefore, is one who actively seeks to align their thoughts, attitudes, and actions with the teachings of Scripture, allowing the Spirit to guide and direct their life.

Being a spiritual person involves more than just outward religiosity or adherence to a set of moral codes. It requires a deep, inward transformation that affects every aspect of one's being. Ephesians 4:23-24 highlights this transformation: "and to be renewed in the spirit of your minds, and to put on the new self, created after the likeness of God in true righteousness and holiness." The renewal of the mind is a continuous process that enables the believer to live in true righteousness and holiness, reflecting the character of God in their daily life.

A spiritual person also prioritizes their relationship with God above all else. Matthew 6:33 instructs, "But seek first the kingdom of God and his righteousness, and all these things will be added to you." This verse underscores the importance of placing God's kingdom and righteousness at the forefront of one's life. A spiritual person is not preoccupied with worldly concerns but is focused on pursuing a deeper relationship with God and fulfilling His will.

Furthermore, being a spiritual person means being sensitive to the leading of the Holy Spirit through the Word of God. Galatians 5:16 advises, "But I say, walk by the Spirit, and you will not gratify the desires of the flesh." Walking by the Spirit involves a daily commitment to follow the guidance of God's Word, resisting the temptations of the flesh, and living in a way that honors God.

How Can We Identify a Spiritual Person?

Identifying a spiritual person involves observing their behavior, attitudes, and priorities in light of Scripture. One of the most significant indicators of a spiritual person is the fruit they bear in their life. Galatians 5:22-23 describes the fruit of the Spirit: "But the fruit of the Spirit is love, joy, peace, patience, kindness, goodness, faithfulness, gentleness, self-control; against such things there is no law." These qualities are the natural outgrowth of a life that is surrendered to God and guided by His Spirit.

A spiritual person is also characterized by humility and a willingness to serve others. Philippians 2:3-4 exhorts, "Do nothing from selfish ambition or conceit, but in humility count others more significant than yourselves. Let each of you look not only to his own interests but also to the interests of others." This passage highlights the selflessness and humility that should define a spiritual person. Rather than seeking their own advantage, a spiritual person is focused on serving others and glorifying God.

Another hallmark of a spiritual person is their devotion to prayer and communion with God. Colossians 4:2 encourages, "Continue steadfastly in prayer, being watchful in it with thanksgiving." A spiritual person recognizes the importance of maintaining a close relationship with God through consistent prayer and thanksgiving. This devotion to prayer is a reflection of their dependence on God and their desire to align their will with His.

A spiritual person is also committed to the study and application of Scripture. Psalm 1:2-3 describes the blessed man as one whose "delight is in the law of Jehovah, and on his law he meditates day and night. He is like a tree planted by streams of water that yields its fruit in its season, and its leaf does not wither. In all that he does, he prospers." A spiritual person delights in God's Word, meditating on it continually and allowing it to shape their thoughts, attitudes, and actions.

Lastly, a spiritual person is marked by their resilience and perseverance in the face of trials. James 1:12 teaches, "Blessed is the man who remains steadfast under trial, for when he has stood the test he will receive the crown of life, which God has promised to those who love him." A spiritual person remains steadfast in their faith, trusting in God's promises and enduring through difficulties with the hope of eternal life.

Maintain Your Faith and Spiritual Health

Maintaining faith and spiritual health is crucial for keeping the mind renewed. Faith, as described in Hebrews 11:1, is "the assurance of things hoped for, the conviction of things not seen." Maintaining faith involves a deep and unwavering trust in God and His promises, even when circumstances seem uncertain or challenging.

One way to maintain faith is through regular engagement with God's Word. Romans 10:17 states, "So faith comes from hearing, and hearing through the word of Christ." The more we immerse ourselves in Scripture, the stronger our faith becomes, as we are continually reminded of God's character, His faithfulness, and His promises. Regular Bible study, meditation, and memorization are essential practices for keeping our faith strong and our minds renewed.

Prayer is another vital component of maintaining faith and spiritual health. Philippians 4:6-7 encourages, "Do not be anxious about anything, but in everything by prayer and supplication with thanksgiving let your requests be made known to God. And the peace of God, which surpasses all understanding, will guard your hearts and your minds in Christ Jesus." Through prayer, we express our dependence on God, seek His guidance, and receive His peace, which strengthens our faith and guards our minds against anxiety and doubt.

Fellowship with other believers is also essential for maintaining faith and spiritual health. Hebrews 10:24-25 instructs, "And let us consider how to stir up one another to love and good works, not neglecting to meet together, as is the habit of some, but encouraging one another, and all the more as you see the Day drawing near." Regular fellowship with other believers provides mutual encouragement, accountability, and support, helping us to stay strong in our faith and focused on living according to God's will.

In addition to these practices, maintaining faith and spiritual health requires a commitment to living out our faith in practical ways. James 2:26 reminds us, "For as the body apart from the spirit is dead, so also faith apart from works is dead." Genuine faith is demonstrated through our actions, as we seek to live out the teachings of Scripture in our daily lives. By serving others, sharing the Gospel, and living in obedience to God's commands, we keep our faith active and vibrant, contributing to the renewal of our minds.

Spirituality and Your Well-Being

Spirituality, when grounded in the truth of Scripture, has a profound impact on our overall well-being. Proverbs 3:5-8 highlights the connection between spiritual health and physical well-being: "Trust in Jehovah with all your heart, and do not lean on your own understanding. In all your ways acknowledge him, and he will make straight your paths. Be not wise in your own eyes; fear Jehovah, and turn away from evil. It will be healing to your flesh and refreshment to your bones." Trusting in God and living according to His Word brings peace, direction, and healing to our lives.

The renewal of the mind through a biblical spirituality contributes to mental and emotional well-being. Philippians 4:8-9 instructs, "Finally, brothers, whatever is true, whatever is honorable, whatever is just, whatever is pure, whatever is lovely, whatever is commendable, if there is any excellence, if there is anything worthy of praise, think about these things. What you have learned and received and heard and seen in me—practice these things, and the God of peace will be with you." By focusing our minds on what is true, honorable, and praiseworthy, we cultivate a positive and peaceful mindset that enhances our emotional and mental health.

Spiritual well-being also affects our relationships with others. Galatians 5:13-14 encourages, "For you were called to freedom, brothers. Only do not use your freedom as an opportunity for the flesh, but through love serve one another. For the whole law is fulfilled in one word: 'You shall love your neighbor as yourself.'" A biblically grounded spirituality fosters love, compassion, and humility in our interactions with others, leading to healthier and more meaningful relationships.

Moreover, spirituality provides a sense of purpose and meaning in life. Ecclesiastes 12:13 concludes, "The end of the matter; all has been heard. Fear God and keep his commandments, for this is the whole duty of man." Living in alignment with God's purpose gives our lives direction and significance, contributing to a sense of fulfillment and well-being.

To maintain spiritual well-being, it is important to engage in practices that nurture our relationship with God and keep our minds renewed. This includes regular prayer, Bible study, fellowship, and service to others. By staying connected to God and living according to His Word, we experience the peace, joy, and purpose that come from a vibrant spiritual life.

Spiritual Dangers in This Wicked World

Living in a world that is increasingly hostile to biblical values presents significant spiritual dangers that can undermine our faith and spiritual health. Ephesians 6:12 warns, "For we do not wrestle against flesh and blood, but against the rulers, against the authorities, against the cosmic powers over this present darkness, against the spiritual forces of evil in the heavenly places." The spiritual battle we face is real, and the enemy seeks to distract, deceive, and destroy our faith.

One of the greatest spiritual dangers in this wicked world is the influence of false teachings and ideologies. 2 Peter 2:1 cautions, "But false prophets also arose among the people, just as there will be false teachers among you, who will secretly bring in destructive heresies, even denying the Master who bought them, bringing upon themselves swift destruction." False teachings can lead believers astray, causing them to abandon the truth of Scripture and embrace beliefs that are contrary to God's Word.

Another spiritual danger is the temptation to conform to the values and practices of the world. Romans 12:2 again exhorts, "Do not be conformed to this world, but be transformed by the renewal of your mind, that by testing you may discern what is the will of God, what is good and acceptable and perfect." The pressure to conform to the world's standards can lead to a compromise of biblical values and a weakening of our faith.

Materialism and the pursuit of worldly success also pose significant spiritual dangers. Matthew 6:24 warns, "No one can serve two masters, for either he will hate the one and love the other, or he will be devoted to the one and despise the other. You cannot serve God and money." The love of money and material possessions can distract us from our devotion to God and lead us away from a life of spiritual significance.

The increasing prevalence of immorality and sin in the world is another spiritual danger. 1 John 2:16 describes the temptations that the world offers: "For all that is in the world—the desires of the flesh and the desires of the eyes and pride of life—is not from the Father but is from the world." Immorality, lust, and pride are rampant in today's culture, and without vigilance, believers can easily fall into these traps.

To protect ourselves from these spiritual dangers, it is essential to stay grounded in the Word of God and maintain a close relationship with Him. Ephesians 6:13-17 advises, "Therefore take up the whole armor of God, that you may be able to withstand in the evil day, and having done all, to stand firm. Stand therefore, having fastened on the belt of truth, and having put on the breastplate of righteousness, and, as shoes for your feet, having put on the readiness given by the gospel of peace. In all circumstances take up the shield of faith, with which you can extinguish all the flaming darts of the evil one; and take the helmet of salvation, and the sword of the Spirit, which is the word of God." By putting on the whole armor of God and staying vigilant, we can stand firm against the spiritual dangers that threaten our faith.

Staying Healthy in Faith

Staying healthy in faith requires intentional effort and discipline, as well as a commitment to nurturing our relationship with God. One of the key ways to maintain spiritual health is through regular engagement with Scripture. Psalm 119:9-11 asks and answers, "How can a young man keep his way pure? By guarding it according to your word. With my whole heart I seek you; let me not wander from your commandments! I have stored up your word in my heart, that I might not sin against you." By storing God's Word in our hearts and living according to it, we keep our faith strong and our lives pure.

Another important aspect of staying healthy in faith is maintaining a consistent prayer life. Luke 18:1 records Jesus' teaching on the necessity of persistent prayer: "And he told them a parable to the effect that they ought always to pray and not lose heart." Persistent prayer keeps us connected to God, strengthens our faith, and helps us navigate the challenges of life with a sense of peace and confidence.

Fellowship with other believers is also essential for staying healthy in faith. Acts 2:42 describes the early church's commitment to fellowship: "And they devoted themselves to the apostles' teaching and the fellowship, to the breaking of bread and the prayers." Regular fellowship provides encouragement, accountability, and support, helping us to stay strong in our faith and live out our commitment to God.

In addition to these practices, staying healthy in faith involves guarding our minds and hearts against the influences of the world. Proverbs 4:23 advises, "Keep your heart with all vigilance, for from it flow the springs of life." By guarding our hearts and minds, we protect ourselves from the corrupting influences of the world and ensure that our faith remains strong and vibrant.

Service to others is another important component of staying healthy in faith. Galatians 6:9 encourages, "And let us not grow weary of doing good, for in due season we will reap, if we do not give up." Serving others not only reflects the love of Christ but also helps to strengthen our faith and keep our focus on what truly matters.

By staying engaged in these spiritual practices and remaining vigilant against the distractions and temptations of the world, we can maintain a healthy and vibrant faith that honors God and keeps our minds renewed.

What Might We Consider When Analyzing Our Spirituality?

When analyzing our spirituality, it is important to reflect on several key areas of our relationship with God and our walk of faith. One of the first areas to consider is our commitment to Scripture. 2 Timothy 2:15 urges, "Do your best to present yourself to God as one approved, a worker who has no need to be ashamed, rightly handling the word of truth." Our approach to Scripture—whether we are diligently studying and applying it—serves as a key indicator of our spiritual health.

Another area to consider is our prayer life. Colossians 4:2 again emphasizes the importance of consistent prayer: "Continue steadfastly in prayer, being watchful in it with thanksgiving." Analyzing our prayer life involves evaluating the consistency, depth, and sincerity of our communication with God. Are we regularly bringing our needs, concerns, and praises before God, and are we seeking His guidance in all areas of our lives?

Our relationships with others are also an important aspect of our spirituality. 1 John 4:7-8 teaches, "Beloved, let us love one another, for love is from God, and whoever loves has been born of God and knows God. Anyone who does not love does not know God, because God is love." Our interactions with others, particularly our ability to love, forgive, and serve, reflect the condition of our spiritual life and our relationship with God.

We should also consider our involvement in the community of believers. Hebrews 10:24-25 again advises, "And let us consider how to stir up one another to love and good works, not neglecting to meet together, as is the habit of some, but encouraging one another, and all the more as you see the Day drawing near." Active participation in the life of the church, including fellowship, worship, and service, is a vital component of a healthy spiritual life.

Our response to trials and challenges is another important area to consider. James 1:2-4 encourages, "Count it all joy, my brothers, when you meet trials of various kinds, for you know that the testing of your faith produces steadfastness. And let steadfastness have its full effect, that you may be perfect and complete, lacking in nothing." How we respond to difficulties—whether with faith, perseverance, and trust in God—reveals much about the depth and maturity of our spirituality.

Finally, we should consider our overall commitment to living a life that honors God. Romans 12:1-2 again exhorts, "I appeal to you therefore, brothers, by the mercies of God, to present your bodies as a living sacrifice, holy and acceptable to God, which is your spiritual worship. Do not be conformed to this world, but be transformed by the renewal of your mind, that by testing you may discern what is the will of God, what is good and acceptable and perfect." Our willingness to sacrifice our own desires, conform to God's will, and live according to His Word is a key indicator of our spiritual health.

What Do We Need to Do to Move Forward as a Spiritual Person?

Moving forward as a spiritual person requires a commitment to continuous growth and a willingness to make necessary changes in our lives. One of the first steps in this process is to prioritize our relationship with God. Matthew 22:37-38 records Jesus' teaching on the greatest commandment: "And he said to him, 'You shall love the Lord your God with all your heart and with all your soul and with all your mind. This is the great and first commandment.'" Loving God with all our heart, soul, and mind means making Him the central focus of our lives and seeking to grow closer to Him every day.

To move forward as a spiritual person, we must also cultivate a habit of regular Bible study and meditation. Psalm 119:15-16 expresses the psalmist's commitment to God's Word: "I will meditate on your precepts and fix my eyes on your ways. I will delight in your statutes; I will not forget your word." By meditating on Scripture and allowing it to guide our thoughts and actions, we align ourselves with God's will and continue to grow in our spiritual journey.

Prayer is another essential practice for moving forward as a spiritual person. Ephesians 6:18 encourages, "praying at all times in the Spirit, with all prayer and supplication. To that end keep alert with all perseverance, making supplication for all the saints." Persistent and heartfelt prayer keeps us connected to God, strengthens our faith, and helps us discern His will in our lives.

Moving forward as a spiritual person also involves being intentional about our relationships with others. Philippians 2:3-4 again advises, "Do nothing from selfish ambition or conceit, but in humility count others more significant than yourselves. Let each of you look not only to his own interests but also to the interests of others." By prioritizing humility, love, and service in our interactions with others, we reflect the character of Christ and contribute to our spiritual growth.

Another important aspect of moving forward as a spiritual person is engaging in regular self-examination. 2 Corinthians 13:5 instructs, "Examine yourselves, to see whether you are in the faith. Test yourselves. Or do you not realize this about yourselves, that Jesus Christ is in you?—unless indeed you fail to meet the test!" Regularly examining our lives, attitudes, and actions in light of Scripture helps us identify areas where we need to grow and make necessary changes.

Finally, moving forward as a spiritual person requires perseverance and a commitment to continuous growth. Philippians 3:12-14 again reflects the apostle Paul's determination to press on in his spiritual journey: "Not that I have already obtained this or am already perfect, but I press on to make it my own, because Christ Jesus has made me his own. Brothers, I do not consider that I have made it my own. But one thing I do: forgetting what lies behind and straining forward to what lies ahead, I press on toward the goal for the prize of the upward call of God in Christ Jesus." By pressing on and striving to grow in our relationship with God, we continue to move forward as spiritual people, living lives that honor Him.

How You Can Satisfy Your Spiritual Needs

Satisfying our spiritual needs requires intentionality and a commitment to nurturing our relationship with God. One of the primary ways to satisfy our spiritual needs is through regular engagement with Scripture. Jesus emphasized the importance of God's Word in Matthew 4:4: "But he answered, 'It is written, "Man shall not live by bread alone, but by every word that comes from the mouth of God."'" Just as physical food sustains our bodies, the Word of God sustains our spirits, providing the nourishment we need to grow and thrive spiritually.

Another essential component of satisfying our spiritual needs is maintaining a consistent prayer life. Psalm 63:1 expresses the psalmist's deep longing for God: "O God, you are my God; earnestly I seek you; my soul thirsts for you; my flesh faints for you, as in a dry and weary land where there is no water." Prayer is a vital means of communion with God, allowing us to express our desires, seek His guidance, and experience His presence.

Fellowship with other believers is also important for satisfying our spiritual needs. Acts 2:42 again highlights the early church's commitment to fellowship: "And they devoted themselves to the apostles' teaching and the fellowship, to the breaking of bread and the prayers." Being part of a community of believers provides mutual encouragement, support, and accountability, helping us to stay strong in our faith and grow spiritually.

Service to others is another way to satisfy our spiritual needs. Jesus taught in Mark 10:45, "For even the Son of Man came not to be served but to serve, and to give his life as a ransom for many." By serving others, we follow the example of Christ and experience the joy and fulfillment that comes from living out our faith in practical ways.

Worship is also an essential aspect of satisfying our spiritual needs. Psalm 95:6-7 invites us to worship God: "Oh come, let us worship and bow down; let us kneel before Jehovah, our Maker! For he is our God, and we are the people of his pasture, and the sheep of his hand."

Worship allows us to express our love and adoration for God, drawing us closer to Him and deepening our relationship with Him.

Finally, satisfying our spiritual needs involves trusting in God's provision and care. Philippians 4:19 assures us, "And my God will supply every need of yours according to his riches in glory in Christ Jesus." By placing our trust in God and relying on His provision, we experience the peace and contentment that come from knowing that our needs—both physical and spiritual—are met in Him.

What Are Innocent Appearing Situations and Why Should We Avoid Them?

Innocent-appearing situations can be deceptive and dangerous, leading us away from God's will and into sin. These situations often appear harmless on the surface but can have subtle, negative influences on our thoughts, attitudes, and actions. Proverbs 14:12 warns, "There is a way that seems right to a man, but its end is the way to death." What may seem innocent or even beneficial at first glance can lead to spiritual harm if it is not in alignment with God's Word.

One example of an innocent-appearing situation is compromising on moral or ethical standards in small ways. These compromises may seem insignificant, but they can lead to a gradual erosion of our spiritual integrity. James 1:14-15 describes the progression of sin: "But each person is tempted when he is lured and enticed by his own desire. Then desire when it has conceived gives birth to sin, and sin when it is fully grown brings forth death." What begins as a small compromise can eventually grow into a pattern of sin that leads to spiritual destruction.

Another example is engaging in entertainment or activities that subtly promote values contrary to Scripture. Philippians 4:8 again encourages us to focus on what is true, honorable, and pure: "Finally, brothers, whatever is true, whatever is honorable, whatever is just, whatever is pure, whatever is lovely, whatever is commendable, if there is any excellence, if there is anything worthy of praise, think about these things." While certain forms of entertainment may seem innocent, they can introduce ideas and values that conflict with biblical truth, leading us away from God's will.

Innocent-appearing situations can also include relationships or associations that influence us in negative ways. 1 Corinthians 15:33 cautions, "Do not be deceived: 'Bad company ruins good morals.'" Even if the influence of others seems subtle, it can still have a significant impact on our spiritual life and lead us into sin.

To avoid the dangers of innocent-appearing situations, it is important to remain vigilant and discerning, relying on God's Word to guide our decisions. Proverbs 4:23-27 advises, "Keep your heart with all vigilance, for from it flow the springs of life. Put away from you crooked speech, and put devious talk far from you. Let your eyes look directly forward, and your gaze be straight before you. Ponder the path of your feet; then all your ways will be sure. Do not swerve to the right or to the left; turn your foot away from evil." By guarding our hearts and minds and staying focused on God's truth, we can avoid the subtle dangers of innocent-appearing situations and live in a way that honors God.

How to Set and Reach the Goal of Being a Spiritual Person?

Setting and reaching the goal of being a spiritual person requires intentional planning, commitment, and reliance on God's grace. The first step in this process is to define what it means to be a spiritual person, grounded in Scripture. As previously discussed, a spiritual person is someone whose life is governed by the Holy Spirit through the Word of God, reflecting the character and values of Christ in every aspect of life.

To set the goal of being a spiritual person, it is important to begin with prayer, asking God for guidance and wisdom. James 1:5 encourages, "If any of you lacks wisdom, let him ask God, who gives generously to all without reproach, and it will be given him." Seeking God's guidance ensures that our goals align with His will and that we rely on His strength to achieve them.

Once the goal is set, it is important to break it down into practical, achievable steps. Philippians 3:13-14 again reflects the apostle Paul's approach to spiritual growth: "Brothers, I do not consider that I have made it my own. But one thing I do: forgetting what lies behind and straining forward to what lies ahead, I press on toward the goal for the prize of the upward call of God in Christ Jesus." By focusing on one step at a time and pressing forward with determination, we can make steady progress toward our goal.

Regular self-examination is also crucial for reaching the goal of being a spiritual person. Lamentations 3:40 advises, "Let us test and examine our ways, and return to Jehovah!" By regularly evaluating our thoughts, attitudes, and actions in light of Scripture, we can identify areas where we need to grow and make necessary adjustments.

Accountability and support from other believers can also help us reach our goal. Ecclesiastes 4:9-10 highlights the value of companionship in the journey of faith: "Two are better than one, because they have a good reward for their toil. For if they fall, one will lift up his fellow. But woe to him who is alone when he falls and has not another to lift him up!" Surrounding ourselves with a community of believers provides encouragement, accountability, and support as we pursue our goal of being a spiritual person.

Finally, reaching the goal of being a spiritual person requires perseverance and trust in God's faithfulness. Galatians 6:9 again encourages, "And let us not grow weary of doing good, for in due season we will reap, if we do not give up." By remaining steadfast in our pursuit of spiritual growth and relying on God's grace, we can reach the goal of being a spiritual person and experience the fullness of life that comes from walking in step with the Holy Spirit.

CHAPTER 6 How Can We Walk in the Light from God?

What Does It Mean to Walk in the Light from God?

Walking in the light from God is a profound biblical concept that signifies living in accordance with the truth, righteousness, and guidance that God provides through His Word. To walk in the light means to live a life that is transparent before God, avoiding the darkness of sin and deception. 1 John 1:5-7 articulates this clearly: "This is the message we have heard from him and proclaim to you, that God is light, and in him is no darkness at all. If we say we have fellowship with him while we walk in darkness, we lie and do not practice the truth. But if we walk in the light, as he is in the light, we have fellowship with one another, and the blood of Jesus his Son cleanses us from all sin."

The imagery of light in Scripture is consistently associated with God's holiness, truth, and purity. In contrast, darkness is associated with sin, ignorance, and evil. Therefore, to walk in the light from God is to live a life that reflects His holiness and truth. This involves rejecting the ways of the world and the works of darkness, and instead, embracing the teachings and commands found in the Bible.

Walking in the light also implies a continual process of growth and transformation. As we expose ourselves to the light of God's Word, we begin to see more clearly the areas of our lives that need to change. Psalm 119:105 declares, "Your word is a lamp to my feet and a light to my path." This verse emphasizes that God's Word provides the guidance and direction we need to walk in His light.

Furthermore, walking in the light from God means living in a manner that is consistent with the character of Christ. Ephesians 5:8-9 exhorts believers: "For at one time you were darkness, but now you are light in the Lord. Walk as children of light (for the fruit of light is found in all that is good and right and true)." This passage highlights the transformative power of walking in the light—believers, once in darkness, are now called to live as children of light, producing the fruit of righteousness.

How Does Walking in the Light Impact Our Relationships with Others?

Walking in the light from God has a profound impact on our relationships with others. When we live in the light, we are called to reflect God's love, truth, and grace in our interactions with others. This involves living transparently, honestly, and lovingly, fostering healthy and godly relationships.

1 John 2:9-10 addresses the connection between walking in the light and our relationships: "Whoever says he is in the light and hates his brother is still in darkness. Whoever loves his brother abides in the light, and in him, there is no cause for stumbling." This passage makes it clear that walking in the light is inseparable from love for others. Hatred, bitterness, or unforgiveness are indicators that a person is still walking in darkness, while love for others is a sign that one is truly walking in the light.

Living in the light also involves being truthful and transparent in our dealings with others. Ephesians 4:25 instructs, "Therefore, having put away falsehood, let each one of you speak the truth with his neighbor, for we are members one of another." When we walk in the light, we reject deceit, dishonesty, and manipulation, choosing instead to speak the truth in love. This fosters trust and unity in our relationships.

Moreover, walking in the light from God means that we are willing to confront sin and wrongdoing in a spirit of love and humility. Galatians 6:1 advises, "Brothers, if anyone is caught in any transgression, you who are spiritual should restore him in a spirit of gentleness. Keep watch on yourself, lest you too be tempted." When we walk in the light, we do not ignore or condone sin, but we address it in a way that seeks restoration and healing, always mindful of our own need for grace.

Walking in the light also enables us to be a positive influence on others. Jesus calls His followers to be the "light of the world" in Matthew 5:14-16: "You are the light of the world. A city set on a hill cannot be hidden. Nor do people light a lamp and put it under a basket, but on a stand, and it gives light to all in the house. In the same way, let your light shine before others, so that they may see your good works and give glory to your Father who is in heaven." By living in the light, we become a testimony to others of God's goodness and truth, drawing them toward Him.

How Can We Remain in the Light from God?

Remaining in the light from God requires intentional and ongoing effort. It is not a one-time decision but a daily commitment to live in alignment with God's will and Word. Here are key ways to remain in the light from God:

Regular Engagement with Scripture: The Word of God is the primary source of light for our lives. Psalm 119:130 states, "The unfolding of your words gives light; it imparts understanding to the simple." By regularly reading, studying, and meditating on Scripture, we keep our minds and hearts aligned with God's truth, which enables us to walk in the light.

Consistent Prayer Life: Prayer is essential for maintaining our relationship with God and staying in His light. Through prayer, we seek God's guidance, confess our sins, and align our will with His. 1 Thessalonians 5:17 exhorts us to "pray without ceasing," indicating the importance of continuous communication with God in our spiritual journey.

Fellowship with Other Believers: Christian fellowship plays a crucial role in helping us remain in the light. Hebrews 10:24-25 advises, "And let us consider how to stir up one another to love and good works, not neglecting to meet together, as is the habit of some, but encouraging one another, and all the more as you see the Day drawing near." Fellowship with other believers provides mutual encouragement, accountability, and support, helping us stay committed to walking in the light.

Obedience to God's Commands: Remaining in the light from God involves obeying His commands and living according to His standards. 1 John 2:3-6 emphasizes, "And by this we know that we have come to know him, if we keep his commandments. Whoever says 'I know him' but does not keep his commandments is a liar, and the truth is not in him, but whoever keeps his word, in him truly the love of God is perfected. By this we may know that we are in him: whoever says he abides in him ought to walk in the same way in which he walked." Obedience is a clear indication that we are walking in the light and remaining in fellowship with God.

Guarding Against Sin and Temptation: Sin can quickly lead us into darkness, so it is vital to guard against it by being vigilant and relying on God's strength. 1 Peter 5:8 warns, "Be sober-minded; be watchful. Your adversary the devil prowls around like a roaring lion, seeking someone to devour." By staying alert and relying on God's Word and the Holy Spirit, we can resist temptation and continue walking in the light.

Confession and Repentance: When we do sin, it is important to quickly confess and repent in order to restore our fellowship with God and remain in His light. 1 John 1:9 assures us, "If we confess our sins, he is faithful and just to forgive us our sins and to cleanse us from all unrighteousness." Confession and repentance are key to maintaining a close relationship with God and walking in the light.

Why Is It Important to Walk in the Light from God?

Walking in the light from God is crucial for several reasons, each of which impacts our spiritual health, our witness to others, and our relationship with God.

First, walking in the light is essential for our spiritual growth and maturity. Ephesians 5:8-10 again encourages believers, "For at one time you were darkness, but now you are light in the Lord. Walk as children of light (for the fruit of light is found in all that is good and right and true), and try to discern what is pleasing to the Lord." When we walk in the light, we grow in righteousness, truth, and goodness, becoming more like Christ in our character and actions.

Second, walking in the light protects us from the deceptions and dangers of sin. Proverbs 4:18-19 contrasts the paths of the righteous and the wicked: "But the path of the righteous is like the light of dawn, which shines brighter and brighter until full day. The way of the wicked is like deep darkness; they do not know over what they stumble." Walking in the light keeps us on the path of righteousness, where we can clearly see and avoid the pitfalls of sin.

Third, walking in the light enhances our fellowship with God and with other believers. 1 John 1:7 emphasizes, "But if we walk in the light, as he is in the light, we have fellowship with one another, and the blood of Jesus his Son cleanses us from all sin." Walking in the light fosters genuine fellowship with God and with others who are also walking in the light. This fellowship is characterized by love, unity, and mutual support.

Fourth, walking in the light is a powerful witness to the world. Jesus calls His followers to be a light in a dark world, as previously noted in Matthew 5:14-16. When we walk in the light, we reflect God's character and truth to those around us, drawing them toward Him. Our lives become a testimony of God's transforming power and a beacon of hope for those who are lost in darkness.

Finally, walking in the light is necessary for our eternal security. 1 John 2:9-11 warns, "Whoever says he is in the light and hates his brother is still in darkness. Whoever loves his brother abides in the light, and in him, there is no cause for stumbling. But whoever hates his brother is in the darkness and walks in the darkness, and does not know where he is going, because the darkness has blinded his eyes." Walking in the light ensures that we remain on the path that leads to eternal life with God, avoiding the dangers of spiritual blindness and separation from Him.

How Do We Reflect the Light of God in Our Daily Lives?

Reflecting the light of God in our daily lives is a practical expression of our walk with Him. This involves living in a way that honors God and points others to Him. Here are some key ways to reflect the light of God:

Living a Life of Integrity: Reflecting the light of God means living with integrity in all areas of our lives. Proverbs 10:9 states, "Whoever walks in integrity walks securely, but he who makes his ways crooked will be found out." Integrity involves being honest, trustworthy, and consistent in our actions, both in public and in private.

Showing Love and Compassion to Others: Jesus taught that love is the greatest commandment, and it is through love that we reflect the light of God to others. John 13:34-35 records Jesus' words, "A new commandment I give to you, that you love one another: just as I have loved you, you also are to love one another. By this, all people will know that you are my disciples if you have love for one another." When we show love and compassion to others, we reflect the love of God and demonstrate that we are His disciples.

Serving Others: Reflecting the light of God also involves serving others selflessly. Galatians 5:13 again exhorts, "For you were called to freedom, brothers. Only do not use your freedom as an opportunity for the flesh, but through love serve one another." Serving others reflects the humility and love of Christ, and it points others to the God who cares for their needs.

Sharing the Gospel: Reflecting the light of God includes sharing the good news of Jesus Christ with others. Matthew 28:19-20 records Jesus' Great Commission: "Go therefore and make disciples of all nations, baptizing them in the name of the Father and of the Son and of the Holy Spirit, teaching them to observe all that I have commanded you. And behold, I am with you always, to the end of the age." By sharing the Gospel, we bring the light of God's truth to those who are in spiritual darkness, offering them the hope of salvation.

PUT OFF THE OLD PERSON

Living with Joy and Hope: The light of God is also reflected in the joy and hope that we exhibit in our daily lives. Romans 15:13 again offers this prayer: "May the God of hope fill you with all joy and peace in believing, so that by the power of the Holy Spirit you may abound in hope." When we live with joy and hope, even in the face of challenges, we reflect the light of God's presence in our lives and testify to His faithfulness.

Resisting Sin and Temptation: Reflecting the light of God also involves resisting sin and living a life of holiness. James 4:7 advises, "Submit yourselves therefore to God. Resist the devil, and he will flee from you." By resisting temptation and choosing to live according to God's Word, we reflect His holiness and purity in our lives.

Practicing Forgiveness: Reflecting the light of God involves practicing forgiveness, just as God has forgiven us. Ephesians 4:32 again instructs, "Be kind to one another, tenderhearted, forgiving one another, as God in Christ forgave you." Forgiveness reflects God's grace and mercy, and it helps to restore and maintain healthy relationships.

Being a Peacemaker: Jesus calls His followers to be peacemakers, reflecting the peace of God in a world filled with conflict. Matthew 5:9 declares, "Blessed are the peacemakers, for they shall be called sons of God." By promoting peace and reconciliation, we reflect the light of God's peace and contribute to the healing of relationships and communities.

Living with Humility: Reflecting the light of God also involves living with humility, recognizing our dependence on Him and placing the needs of others above our own. Philippians 2:3-4 again exhorts, "Do nothing from selfish ambition or conceit, but in humility count others more significant than yourselves. Let each of you look not only to his own interests but also to the interests of others." Humility reflects the character of Christ and points others to the God who exalts the humble.

How Can We Guard Against Falling Back into Darkness?

While walking in the light from God, it is important to remain vigilant and guard against the dangers of falling back into darkness. The Bible provides several strategies to help us stay on the path of light and avoid the pitfalls of sin and spiritual darkness.

Regular Self-Examination: Regularly examining our lives in light of Scripture helps us identify areas where we may be drifting toward darkness. 2 Corinthians 13:5 again advises, "Examine yourselves, to see whether you are in the faith. Test yourselves. Or do you not realize this about yourselves, that Jesus Christ is in you?—unless indeed you fail to meet the test!" By regularly evaluating our thoughts, actions, and attitudes, we can address any areas of concern and make necessary adjustments to stay in the light.

Confession and Repentance: When we do sin, it is crucial to quickly confess and repent to restore our fellowship with God and remain in the light. 1 John 1:9 again assures us, "If we confess our sins, he is faithful and just to forgive us our sins and to cleanse us from all unrighteousness." Confession and repentance keep our hearts and minds aligned with God's will, preventing us from falling back into darkness.

Accountability: Having accountability partners—trusted fellow believers who can encourage, challenge, and support us—helps us stay on the path of light. Hebrews 3:13 advises, "But exhort one another every day, as long as it is called 'today,' that none of you may be hardened by the deceitfulness of sin." Accountability relationships provide mutual encouragement and help us resist the temptations that could lead us back into darkness.

Staying Connected to God's Word: Regular engagement with Scripture is essential for staying in the light and guarding against darkness. Psalm 119:11 again declares, "I have stored up your word in my heart, that I might not sin against you." By continually immersing ourselves in God's Word, we keep our minds and hearts focused on His truth, which helps us resist the lies and deceptions of the enemy.

Prayer: Consistent prayer is vital for maintaining our connection with God and staying in the light. Matthew 26:41 records Jesus' instruction to His disciples: "Watch and pray that you may not enter into temptation. The spirit indeed is willing, but the flesh is weak." Prayer strengthens our resolve to walk in the light and provides the spiritual fortitude needed to resist temptation.

Fleeing from Temptation: When faced with temptation, the Bible instructs us to flee from it rather than entertain it. 1 Corinthians 10:13 assures us, "No temptation has overtaken you that is not common to man. God is faithful, and he will not let you be tempted beyond your ability, but with the temptation he will also provide the way of escape, that you may be able to endure it." By fleeing from temptation and seeking God's way of escape, we protect ourselves from falling back into darkness.

Maintaining Fellowship with Other Believers: Regular fellowship with other believers helps us stay encouraged and accountable in our walk with God. Hebrews 10:24-25 again emphasizes the importance of fellowship: "And let us consider how to stir up one another to love and good works, not neglecting to meet together, as is the habit of some, but encouraging one another, and all the more as you see the Day drawing near." Being part of a supportive Christian community provides the encouragement and strength needed to remain in the light.

Guarding Our Hearts and Minds: Proverbs 4:23 again advises, "Keep your heart with all vigilance, for from it flow the springs of life." Guarding our hearts and minds involves being mindful of what we allow to influence us, whether through media, relationships, or environments. By filtering out negative influences and focusing on what is pure and true, we protect ourselves from the darkness.

Living with an Eternal Perspective: Keeping our eyes fixed on the eternal rewards of walking in the light helps us stay motivated and committed to the path of righteousness. Colossians 3:1-2 again encourages, "If then you have been raised with Christ, seek the things that are above, where Christ is, seated at the right hand of God. Set your minds on things that are above, not on things that are on earth."

By focusing on the eternal rather than the temporal, we remain steadfast in our commitment to walking in the light.

Seeking God's Strength: Finally, we must always rely on God's strength rather than our own to walk in the light and resist darkness. Philippians 4:13 declares, "I can do all things through him who strengthens me." By relying on God's strength and grace, we can overcome the challenges and temptations we face and remain in the light.

Walking in the light from God is a lifelong journey that requires continuous effort, vigilance, and dependence on God. By following these biblical principles and remaining committed to our relationship with God, we can successfully walk in the light, reflecting His glory and avoiding the dangers of spiritual darkness.

CHAPTER 7 What Is the Mind of Christ?

The Human Side of Jesus: What Was Jesus Like as a Person?

Understanding the mind of Christ requires us first to appreciate the human side of Jesus, as He walked the earth in a manner that perfectly embodied the principles and character of God. The Scriptures present Jesus as both fully divine and fully human, a truth that underscores His ability to relate to us in our struggles and triumphs. Philippians 2:5-7 encapsulates this mystery: "Have this mind among yourselves, which is yours in Christ Jesus, who, though he was in the form of God, did not count equality with God a thing to be grasped, but emptied himself, by taking the form of a servant, being born in the likeness of men." This passage highlights the humility and servanthood of Jesus, characteristics that define His mindset and actions.

Jesus' humanity is evident in the emotions He expressed, the relationships He formed, and the life He lived. Far from being aloof or detached, Jesus was deeply connected to those around Him, showing compassion, empathy, and love. In John 11:35, the shortest verse in the Bible, we see a profound expression of His humanity: "Jesus wept." This moment at the tomb of Lazarus reveals not only Jesus' deep sorrow at the death of a friend but also His empathy for the grief of others. His tears were not just for Lazarus but for the pain that death brings to all humanity.

Jesus was also a man of joy, as demonstrated by His interactions with people of all walks of life. He celebrated with others, such as at the wedding in Cana (John 2:1-11), and He often used feasts and meals as opportunities to teach and fellowship with others. His joy was not superficial, but rooted in the deep understanding of God's love and His mission on earth.

Moreover, Jesus was a man of sorrow, as Isaiah 53:3 foretells: "He was despised and rejected by men; a man of sorrows, and acquainted with grief; and as one from whom men hide their faces he was despised, and we esteemed him not." Jesus experienced rejection, betrayal, and physical suffering, all of which He endured with the knowledge that it was necessary for the salvation of humanity.

Jesus' humanity was also reflected in His need for rest and solitude. Mark 1:35 tells us, "And rising very early in the morning, while it was still dark, he departed and went out to a desolate place, and there he prayed." Despite the demands of His ministry, Jesus prioritized time alone with God, modeling the importance of spiritual renewal and communion with the Father.

A Man of Courage, A Man of Feelings, A Bold Man of Action

Jesus' courage is a central aspect of His character. He was unafraid to confront injustice, hypocrisy, and sin, even when it placed Him in direct opposition to the religious leaders of His day. In Matthew 23, Jesus boldly condemns the scribes and Pharisees, calling them out for their hypocrisy and leading the people astray. His courage was not born out of a desire to provoke, but out of His unwavering commitment to truth and righteousness.

Jesus also displayed profound courage in His actions, particularly in His willingness to embrace the cross. Knowing full well the suffering that awaited Him, Jesus did not shrink back but instead resolutely set His face toward Jerusalem (Luke 9:51). His prayer in the Garden of Gethsemane, recorded in Matthew 26:39, reveals the depth of His resolve: "And going a little farther he fell on his face and prayed, saying, 'My Father, if it be possible, let this cup pass from me; nevertheless, not as I will, but as you will.'" Jesus' courage was rooted in His submission to the Father's will, even unto death.

In addition to courage, Jesus was a man of deep feelings. He was not stoic or detached but fully engaged with the emotions and experiences of those around Him. For instance, in Mark 10:21, when a rich young man approached Jesus asking how he might inherit eternal life, the text says, "And Jesus, looking at him, loved him." Jesus' love for the man was evident, even though He knew that the man would struggle to give up his wealth to follow Him. Jesus' emotions were always aligned with the will of God, reflecting a perfect balance of love, compassion, and righteous indignation.

Jesus was also a bold man of action. He did not merely teach with words but demonstrated His teachings through His deeds. One of the most striking examples of this is found in John 13, where Jesus washes the feet of His disciples. This act of humility was shocking to His followers, as washing feet was a task reserved for the lowest of servants. Yet, Jesus performed this act to demonstrate that true greatness in the kingdom of God is found in service, not in power or position.

Jesus' boldness extended to His miracles, which were often performed publicly and in direct defiance of the religious leaders' expectations. For example, in John 9, Jesus heals a man born blind on the Sabbath, an act that sparked outrage among the Pharisees. Yet, Jesus was unapologetic, emphasizing that His work was to do the will of the Father, regardless of the consequences.

Let the Children Come to Me

Jesus' interaction with children provides a profound insight into His character and the mind of Christ. In a culture where children were often seen as insignificant, Jesus elevated their status, showing that they held a special place in the kingdom of God. In Matthew 19:13-14, we read, "Then children were brought to him that he might lay his hands on them and pray. The disciples rebuked the people, but Jesus said, 'Let the little children come to me and do not hinder them, for to such belongs the kingdom of heaven.'"

This statement is powerful for several reasons. First, it shows that Jesus valued and welcomed those whom society often overlooked. His embrace of children symbolized His broader mission to reach out to the marginalized, the weak, and the vulnerable. Jesus saw in children the qualities that are essential for entering the kingdom of heaven: humility, dependence, and trust.

Second, Jesus' invitation to the children serves as a model for how we should approach Him. Like children, we are called to come to Jesus with a sense of wonder, openness, and receptivity. Jesus did not see children as a distraction or a nuisance but as an integral part of His ministry. This teaches us that in the kingdom of God, there is no one too small or insignificant to be valued and loved.

Moreover, Jesus' treatment of children is a reminder of the importance of nurturing faith from a young age. In Deuteronomy 6:6-7, the Israelites are instructed, "And these words that I command you today shall be on your heart. You shall teach them diligently to your children, and shall talk of them when you sit in your house, and when you walk by the way, and when you lie down, and when you rise." Jesus exemplified this principle by welcoming children into His presence, blessing them, and affirming their worth in the eyes of God.

Jesus' Dealings with Women

Jesus' interactions with women were revolutionary for His time, challenging the cultural norms and demonstrating the inclusive nature of the kingdom of God. In a society where women were often marginalized and treated as second-class citizens, Jesus showed them dignity, respect, and compassion.

One of the most striking examples of this is found in John 4, where Jesus speaks with the Samaritan woman at the well. In this encounter, Jesus breaks several societal taboos: He speaks to a woman in public, engages with a Samaritan (a group despised by the Jews), and addresses her past without condemnation. John 4:9-10 records the exchange: "The Samaritan woman said to him, 'How is it that you, a Jew, ask for a drink from me, a woman of Samaria?' (For Jews have no dealings with Samaritans.) Jesus answered her, 'If you knew the gift of God, and who it is that is saying to you, "Give me a drink," you would have asked him, and he would have given you living water.'"

This interaction highlights several key aspects of Jesus' dealings with women. First, He sees beyond societal labels and prejudices, recognizing the inherent worth of every individual. Second, He engages with women on a deep, spiritual level, offering them the same opportunities for growth and transformation as He offers to men. Third, He empowers women to share the message of the Gospel, as the Samaritan woman goes on to become a witness to her entire town (John 4:39).

Another example is Jesus' interaction with the woman caught in adultery, as recorded in John 8:3-11. The religious leaders bring the woman before Jesus, hoping to trap Him by forcing Him to choose between the law of Moses and His message of grace. Instead of condemning the woman, Jesus turns the situation back on her accusers, saying, "Let him who is without sin among you be the first to throw a stone at her." One by one, the accusers leave, and Jesus tells the woman, "Neither do I condemn you; go, and from now on sin no more."

In this encounter, Jesus demonstrates His commitment to justice and mercy. He does not excuse the woman's sin but offers her a path to redemption. His dealings with women are marked by a balance of truth and grace, affirming their value while calling them to a higher standard of living.

Jesus' Relationship with His Disciples: He Expressed Belief in His Disciples

Jesus' relationship with His disciples is a testament to His ability to see potential in others, even when they could not see it in themselves. Throughout the Gospels, we see Jesus patiently teaching, correcting, and encouraging His disciples, even when they struggled to understand His message or faltered in their faith.

One of the most profound examples of Jesus' belief in His disciples is found in Matthew 16:18, where He says to Peter, "And I tell you, you are Peter, and on this rock I will build my church, and the gates of hell shall not prevail against it." Despite Peter's impulsiveness and later denial of Jesus, Jesus saw in him the potential to be a foundational leader in the early church. Jesus' words to Peter were not just a declaration of what Peter would become, but an affirmation of the faith Jesus had in His disciple's ability to fulfill his calling.

Jesus also expressed belief in His disciples by entrusting them with significant responsibilities. In Luke 10:1-2, Jesus sends out seventy-two disciples to preach the kingdom of God and heal the sick: "After this, the Lord appointed seventy-two others and sent them on ahead of him, two by two, into every town and place where he himself was about to go. And he said to them, 'The harvest is plentiful, but the laborers are few. Therefore pray earnestly to the Lord of the harvest to send out laborers into his harvest.'" Jesus' confidence in His disciples' ability to carry out His mission reflects His belief in their potential and the empowerment that comes from following Him.

Moreover, Jesus' post-resurrection appearances to His disciples further demonstrate His belief in them. In John 20:21-22, Jesus says to His disciples, "Peace be with you. As the Father has sent me, even so I am sending you." And when he had said this, he breathed on them and said to them, 'Receive the Holy Spirit.'" Despite their earlier doubts and fears, Jesus commissions them to continue His work, showing that He believes they are capable of carrying out the mission He started.

Easy to Approach

One of the most remarkable aspects of Jesus' ministry was His approachability. Unlike the religious leaders of His time, who often distanced themselves from the common people, Jesus was accessible to all. Whether it was a tax collector, a leper, or a child, Jesus welcomed everyone who came to Him.

Matthew 11:28-30 captures Jesus' open invitation: "Come to me, all who labor and are heavy laden, and I will give you rest. Take my yoke upon you, and learn from me, for I am gentle and lowly in heart, and you will find rest for your souls. For my yoke is easy, and my burden is light." This passage reflects Jesus' desire to provide comfort and relief to those who are burdened by life's challenges. His gentleness and humility made Him easy to approach, and His willingness to meet people where they were at, regardless of their status or background, drew many to Him.

Jesus' approachability is also evident in His interactions with those who were marginalized by society. In Mark 1:40-42, we read of a leper who approached Jesus, saying, "If you will, you can make me clean." Jesus, moved with pity, stretched out His hand and touched him, saying, "I will; be clean." The fact that Jesus touched the leper, a person who was considered unclean and untouchable, highlights His compassion and willingness to break societal norms to show love and acceptance.

Jesus' approachability extended to those who were considered sinners. In Luke 19:1-10, Jesus invites Himself to the house of Zacchaeus, a chief tax collector who was despised by the people. Despite the grumbling of the crowd, Jesus sees Zacchaeus' desire to change and declares, "Today salvation has come to this house, since he also is a son of Abraham. For the Son of Man came to seek and to save the lost." Jesus' willingness to associate with sinners and outcasts demonstrates that He was approachable to all, regardless of their past or their social standing.

Learn From Christ's Mild Temperament

Jesus' mild temperament is another key aspect of His character that reveals the mind of Christ. While He was capable of righteous anger, as seen when He cleansed the temple (John 2:13-17), Jesus was generally characterized by gentleness and self-control. His mildness was not a sign of weakness, but of strength under control—a quality that allowed Him to respond to others with patience and kindness, even in the face of provocation.

In Matthew 12:18-20, the fulfillment of Isaiah's prophecy about the Servant of Jehovah speaks to Jesus' mildness: "Behold, my servant whom I have chosen, my beloved with whom my soul is well pleased. I will put my Spirit upon him, and he will proclaim justice to the Gentiles. He will not quarrel or cry aloud, nor will anyone hear his voice in the streets; a bruised reed he will not break, and a smoldering wick he will not quench, until he brings justice to victory." This passage highlights Jesus' gentle approach to bringing justice—He did not seek to impose His will through force or violence, but through quiet strength and persistence.

Jesus' mildness is also evident in how He dealt with His disciples' misunderstandings and failures. For example, in Luke 22:24-27, the disciples argue about who among them is the greatest. Instead of rebuking them harshly, Jesus gently redirects their focus, saying, "The kings of the Gentiles exercise lordship over them, and those in authority over them are called benefactors. But not so with you. Rather, let the greatest among you become as the youngest, and the leader as one who serves." Jesus' response reflects His mildness and His desire to teach His disciples through patience and example rather than through harsh criticism.

Moreover, Jesus' mild temperament was evident in His interactions with those who were seeking healing or forgiveness. In Matthew 9:20-22, a woman who had been suffering from a bleeding disorder for twelve years approached Jesus, believing that if she only touched His cloak, she would be healed. Jesus, aware of her faith, turned to her and said, "Take heart, daughter; your faith has made you well." And instantly the woman was made well." Jesus' gentle and affirming words highlight His compassion and sensitivity to the needs of those who sought Him.

Jesus Treated Others with Kindness: Show Kindness in an Unkind World

Jesus' kindness was a defining characteristic of His ministry. In a world that was often harsh and unforgiving, Jesus consistently showed kindness to those He encountered, regardless of their social status, background, or circumstances. His kindness was not limited to acts of charity but was deeply rooted in His love for humanity and His desire to reflect the Father's heart.

One of the most poignant examples of Jesus' kindness is found in Luke 7:11-15, where He encounters a funeral procession for the only son of a widow. Moved by compassion, Jesus approaches the widow and says, "Do not weep." Then He touches the bier and says, "Young man, I say to you, arise." The young man sits up and begins to speak, and Jesus gives him back to his mother. Jesus' kindness in this situation is evident in His willingness to interrupt a funeral procession to bring comfort and hope to a grieving mother.

Jesus also showed kindness to those who were ostracized by society. In Luke 5:12-13, a man full of leprosy approaches Jesus and says, "Lord, if you will, you can make me clean." Jesus stretches out His hand and touches him, saying, "I will; be clean." And immediately the leprosy leaves him. Jesus' kindness is evident not only in His willingness to heal the man but also in His touch—a gesture that communicated acceptance and love to someone who had likely been shunned for years.

In addition, Jesus' kindness extended to those who were considered His enemies. In Matthew 5:43-44, Jesus teaches, "You have heard that it was said, 'You shall love your neighbor and hate your enemy.' But I say to you, Love your enemies and pray for those who persecute you." Jesus exemplified this teaching throughout His ministry, most notably on the cross, where He prayed for those who were crucifying Him: "Father, forgive them, for they know not what they do" (Luke 23:34). Jesus' kindness in the face of such cruelty is a powerful example of the depth of His love and His commitment to reflecting the heart of God.

Jesus Was Considerate of Others, Willing to Trust Others

Jesus' consideration for others was evident in the way He interacted with people, always taking into account their needs, feelings, and circumstances. His willingness to trust others, even when they were flawed or imperfect, reflects His belief in the potential for growth and transformation in every person.

In Mark 6:31, after a period of intense ministry, Jesus recognizes the need for His disciples to rest: "And he said to them, 'Come away by yourselves to a desolate place and rest a while.' For many were coming and going, and they had no leisure even to eat." Jesus' consideration for the physical and emotional well-being of His disciples shows His understanding of their humanity and His care for their needs.

Jesus was also considerate in how He approached those who were hurting or in need. In John 8:3-11, when the woman caught in adultery is brought before Him, Jesus takes into account not only the legal aspects of the situation but also the woman's dignity and worth. Instead of condemning her, He challenges her accusers and offers her a path to redemption, saying, "Neither do I condemn you; go, and from now on sin no more."

Moreover, Jesus' willingness to trust others is seen in His relationship with His disciples. Despite their weaknesses and failures, Jesus entrusted them with the mission of spreading the Gospel. In Matthew 28:19-20, He commissions them, saying, "Go therefore and make disciples of all nations, baptizing them in the name of the Father and of the Son and of the Holy Spirit, teaching them to observe all that I have commanded you. And behold, I am with you always, to the end of the age." Jesus' trust in His disciples reflects His belief in their ability to carry out His mission, empowered by the Holy Spirit.

Jesus' consideration for others and His willingness to trust them also extend to His followers today. He invites us to take part in His mission, trusting that we, too, can grow and be transformed as we walk in His ways.

Keep Christ's Mental Attitude in You

The mind of Christ is characterized by humility, obedience, love, and a deep commitment to doing the will of the Father. Philippians 2:5-8 urges believers to adopt the same mindset: "Have this mind among yourselves, which is yours in Christ Jesus, who, though he was in the form of God, did not count equality with God a thing to be grasped, but emptied himself, by taking the form of a servant, being born in the likeness of men. And being found in human form, he humbled himself by becoming obedient to the point of death, even death on a cross."

To keep Christ's mental attitude in us, we must first cultivate humility. Jesus' humility is evident in His willingness to take on human flesh, to serve others, and to submit to the Father's will, even when it led to the cross. Humility involves recognizing our dependence on God and our need to prioritize others above ourselves, as Jesus did.

Second, obedience is a hallmark of the mind of Christ. Jesus was fully committed to obeying the Father's will, regardless of the cost. In John 6:38, Jesus says, "For I have come down from heaven, not to do my own will but the will of him who sent me." Keeping Christ's mental attitude means aligning our will with God's and being willing to follow His commands, even when it is difficult or inconvenient.

Third, love is central to the mind of Christ. Jesus' love for humanity was the driving force behind His ministry, His teachings, and ultimately, His sacrifice on the cross. John 13:34-35 records Jesus' command to His disciples: "A new commandment I give to you, that you love one another: just as I have loved you, you also are to love one another. By this, all people will know that you are my disciples if you have love for one another." To keep Christ's mental attitude, we must cultivate a love that is selfless, sacrificial, and reflective of the love that Jesus has for us.

Finally, keeping Christ's mental attitude involves a deep commitment to God's truth and a willingness to stand firm in the face of opposition. Jesus was unwavering in His commitment to the truth, even when it led to conflict with the religious leaders of His day. In John 14:6, Jesus declares, "I am the way, and the truth, and the life. No one comes to the Father except through me." As followers of Christ, we are called to hold fast to His truth, even when it is countercultural or unpopular.

In conclusion, the mind of Christ is the model for how we are to live as His followers. By embracing humility, obedience, love, and truth, we can keep Christ's mental attitude in us, reflecting His character and carrying out His mission in the world. This requires ongoing spiritual growth, a commitment to God's Word, and a reliance on the Holy Spirit to transform us into the image of Christ.

CHAPTER 8 How Can We Address Spiritual Sicknesses of Mind and Heart?

Having the Right Mind

A healthy spiritual life begins with having the right mind—a mind that is aligned with God's truth and guided by His Word. The mind plays a crucial role in our spiritual well-being, as it is the seat of our thoughts, attitudes, and decisions. Romans 12:2 emphasizes the importance of renewing the mind: "Do not be conformed to this world, but be transformed by the renewal of your mind, that by testing you may discern what is the will of God, what is good and acceptable and perfect."

To have the right mind, we must first fill it with the truth of God's Word. Colossians 3:16 instructs, "Let the word of Christ dwell in you richly, teaching and admonishing one another in all wisdom, singing psalms and hymns and spiritual songs, with thankfulness in your hearts to God." By immersing ourselves in Scripture, we allow God's truth to shape our thoughts and attitudes, enabling us to resist the lies and deceptions of the world.

A right mind is also characterized by humility and a willingness to submit to God's will. Philippians 2:5-7 again reminds us to have the same mindset as Christ: "Have this mind among yourselves, which is yours in Christ Jesus, who, though he was in the form of God, did not count equality with God a thing to be grasped, but emptied himself, by taking the form of a servant, being born in the likeness of men." Jesus' humility and submission to the Father's will serve as the ultimate example for us as we seek to align our minds with God's purposes.

Additionally, a right mind is marked by discernment. In a world filled with conflicting messages and ideologies, it is essential to develop the ability to discern between truth and falsehood. Hebrews 5:14

highlights the importance of discernment: "But solid food is for the mature, for those who have their powers of discernment trained by constant practice to distinguish good from evil." Through the regular study of Scripture and reliance on the Holy Spirit's guidance, we can sharpen our discernment and make decisions that honor God.

To maintain the right mind, we must also guard against negative influences that can corrupt our thinking. Philippians 4:8 again offers this exhortation: "Finally, brothers, whatever is true, whatever is honorable, whatever is just, whatever is pure, whatever is lovely, whatever is commendable, if there is any excellence, if there is anything worthy of praise, think about these things." By focusing on what is pure and noble, we protect our minds from being polluted by worldly influences.

Having the Right Heart

Just as the mind is central to our spiritual health, so too is the heart. The Bible often uses the term "heart" to refer to the innermost part of a person, encompassing emotions, desires, and intentions. Proverbs 4:23 warns, "Keep your heart with all vigilance, for from it flow the springs of life." This verse underscores the importance of guarding our hearts, as the condition of our hearts directly impacts our spiritual health and the direction of our lives.

A right heart is one that is fully devoted to God. Deuteronomy 6:5 commands, "You shall love Jehovah your God with all your heart and with all your soul and with all your might." Loving God with all our heart means placing Him at the center of our lives, allowing His love to shape our desires, motives, and actions.

A right heart is also characterized by purity. Psalm 51:10 expresses a heartfelt prayer for purity: "Create in me a clean heart, O God, and renew a right spirit within me." Recognizing our need for God's cleansing and renewal is essential for maintaining a pure heart. When we confess our sins and seek God's forgiveness, He purifies our hearts and restores our fellowship with Him.

Moreover, a right heart is one that is responsive to God's leading. In Ezekiel 36:26-27, God promises to give His people a new heart:

"And I will give you a new heart, and a new spirit I will put within you. And I will remove the heart of stone from your flesh and give you a heart of flesh. And I will put my Spirit within you, and cause you to walk in my statutes and be careful to obey my rules." This transformation of the heart enables us to respond to God's commands with obedience and joy.

To cultivate a right heart, we must also practice humility and repentance. James 4:8-10 exhorts us, "Draw near to God, and he will draw near to you. Cleanse your hands, you sinners, and purify your hearts, you double-minded. Be wretched and mourn and weep. Let your laughter be turned to mourning and your joy to gloom. Humble yourselves before the Lord, and he will exalt you." A heart that is humble and repentant is open to God's correction and is willing to be shaped by His hands.

How Satan and His World Try to Infect Your Mind and Heart

Satan is a master deceiver, and one of his primary strategies is to infect our minds and hearts with lies, doubts, and sinful desires. Jesus refers to Satan as the "father of lies" in John 8:44: "You are of your father the devil, and your will is to do your father's desires. He was a murderer from the beginning, and does not stand in the truth, because there is no truth in him. When he lies, he speaks out of his own character, for he is a liar and the father of lies." By distorting the truth and planting seeds of doubt, Satan seeks to lead us away from God and into spiritual sickness.

One of the ways Satan attacks our minds is through the subtle introduction of false teachings and philosophies that contradict Scripture. Colossians 2:8 warns, "See to it that no one takes you captive by philosophy and empty deceit, according to human tradition, according to the elemental spirits of the world, and not according to Christ." These false teachings may appear attractive or logical, but they ultimately lead us away from the truth and into spiritual bondage.

Satan also seeks to infect our hearts with bitterness, anger, and unforgiveness. Ephesians 4:26-27 cautions, "Be angry and do not sin;

do not let the sun go down on your anger, and give no opportunity to the devil." When we harbor negative emotions and refuse to forgive, we open the door for Satan to take advantage of our vulnerabilities and lead us into further spiritual decay.

Another tactic Satan uses is to tempt us with the desires of the flesh, the lust of the eyes, and the pride of life. 1 John 2:16 again describes these worldly temptations: "For all that is in the world—the desires of the flesh and the desires of the eyes and pride of life—is not from the Father but is from the world." By appealing to our sinful nature, Satan attempts to draw us away from God and into a life dominated by selfish desires and worldly pursuits.

In addition to these strategies, Satan seeks to isolate us from the fellowship of believers, knowing that we are more vulnerable to his attacks when we are alone. 1 Peter 5:8 warns, "Be sober-minded; be watchful. Your adversary the devil prowls around like a roaring lion, seeking someone to devour." Just as a predator targets the isolated and weak, Satan targets those who are cut off from the support and encouragement of the Christian community.

How to Heal Sicknesses of Mind and Heart

Healing from spiritual sickness requires a deliberate and holistic approach that addresses both the mind and the heart. The first step toward healing is acknowledging the presence of spiritual sickness and confessing it before God. Psalm 32:5 highlights the importance of confession: "I acknowledged my sin to you, and I did not cover my iniquity; I said, 'I will confess my transgressions to Jehovah,' and you forgave the iniquity of my sin." Confession brings our spiritual sickness into the light, where it can be addressed by God's grace and mercy.

Following confession, repentance is crucial for healing. Repentance involves turning away from the sin that has infected our mind and heart and turning back to God. Acts 3:19-20 urges, "Repent therefore, and turn back, that your sins may be blotted out, that times of refreshing may come from the presence of the Lord." Repentance leads to spiritual renewal and refreshment as we realign our lives with God's will.

Another key aspect of healing is immersing ourselves in God's Word. Hebrews 4:12 describes the Word of God as "living and active, sharper than any two-edged sword, piercing to the division of soul and of spirit, of joints and of marrow, and discerning the thoughts and intentions of the heart." Scripture has the power to expose and heal the root causes of spiritual sickness, providing the guidance and wisdom we need to live in accordance with God's truth.

Prayer is also essential for healing spiritual sicknesses of mind and heart. James 5:16 encourages believers to pray for one another: "Therefore, confess your sins to one another and pray for one another, that you may be healed. The prayer of a righteous person has great power as it is working." Through prayer, we invite God's healing presence into our lives and seek His strength to overcome the spiritual sickness that has taken hold.

In addition to personal prayer, seeking the support and encouragement of fellow believers is vital for healing. Galatians 6:2 exhorts, "Bear one another's burdens, and so fulfill the law of Christ." The Christian community provides a network of support where we can find accountability, encouragement, and practical help as we pursue healing and spiritual health.

Finally, healing requires a commitment to ongoing spiritual growth and maturity. Ephesians 4:15 calls us to "grow up in every way into him who is the head, into Christ." As we grow in our relationship with Christ and deepen our understanding of His Word, we become more resilient against spiritual sickness and better equipped to maintain a healthy mind and heart.

You Can Avoid a Spiritual Heart Attack

Just as physical heart attacks can be prevented through healthy living, spiritual heart attacks can be avoided by maintaining a healthy spiritual life. One of the most effective ways to prevent a spiritual heart attack is to regularly examine our hearts before God, allowing Him to reveal any areas of concern. Psalm 139:23-24 is a powerful prayer of examination: "Search me, O God, and know my heart! Try me and know my thoughts! And see if there be any grievous way in me, and lead me in the way everlasting!" Regular self-examination helps us identify and address spiritual issues before they become critical.

Another way to prevent a spiritual heart attack is to guard against bitterness, unforgiveness, and other negative emotions that can poison our hearts. Hebrews 12:15 warns, "See to it that no one fails to obtain the grace of God; that no 'root of bitterness' springs up and causes trouble, and by it, many become defiled." By dealing with these emotions promptly and seeking reconciliation where needed, we protect our hearts from becoming hardened and calloused.

Maintaining a strong prayer life is also crucial for avoiding a spiritual heart attack. In Luke 18:1, Jesus teaches the importance of persistent prayer: "And he told them a parable to the effect that they ought always to pray and not lose heart." Through regular prayer, we stay connected to God, receive His guidance, and strengthen our hearts against spiritual attacks.

Moreover, staying grounded in God's Word is essential for keeping our hearts healthy. Psalm 119:11 again declares, "I have stored up your word in my heart, that I might not sin against you." By regularly reading, meditating on, and applying Scripture, we fill our hearts with God's truth, which acts as a safeguard against spiritual disease.

Finally, surrounding ourselves with godly influences and avoiding toxic environments helps prevent a spiritual heart attack. Proverbs 4:14-15 advises, "Do not enter the path of the wicked, and do not walk in the way of the evil. Avoid it; do not go on it; turn away from it and pass on." By choosing our associations and environments wisely, we reduce our exposure to influences that could lead us into spiritual danger.

Do Not Ignore Warning Signs of an Infected Mind and Heart

Just as physical illness often presents warning signs, so too do spiritual sicknesses of mind and heart. It is crucial not to ignore these signs, as doing so can lead to more serious spiritual problems.

One of the most common warning signs of an infected mind is a loss of interest in spiritual matters. When we find ourselves becoming indifferent or apathetic toward prayer, Scripture, and fellowship with other believers, it may indicate that our mind has been infected by worldly influences. Revelation 2:4-5 warns the church in Ephesus of this danger: "But I have this against you, that you have abandoned the love you had at first. Remember therefore from where you have fallen; repent, and do the works you did at first." Recognizing and addressing spiritual apathy is essential for restoring our passion for God.

Another warning sign is the presence of persistent negative thoughts, such as doubt, fear, or bitterness. These thoughts can be symptoms of a mind that has been infected by lies and deceptions. 2 Corinthians 10:5 instructs, "We destroy arguments and every lofty opinion raised against the knowledge of God, and take every thought captive to obey Christ." By identifying and rejecting negative thoughts, we can prevent them from taking root and causing further spiritual damage.

For the heart, warning signs of infection may include a lack of compassion, an inability to forgive, or a tendency toward selfishness. 1 John 3:17-18 challenges believers: "But if anyone has the world's goods and sees his brother in need, yet closes his heart against him, how does God's love abide in him? Little children, let us not love in word or talk but in deed and in truth." A heart that has become hardened or closed off to others is a sign that spiritual sickness has set in.

Ignoring these warning signs can lead to spiritual burnout, disillusionment, or even a complete falling away from the faith. Hebrews 3:12 again warns, "Take care, brothers, lest there be in any of you an evil, unbelieving heart, leading you to fall away from the living

God." It is vital to address these issues promptly by seeking God's help through prayer, confession, and repentance.

Spiritual Dangers in This Sick World and Outside Sources of Spiritual Disease

The world we live in is filled with spiritual dangers that can infect our minds and hearts if we are not vigilant. These dangers come in many forms, from the pervasive influence of secular culture to the subtle allure of materialism and the constant pressure to conform to societal norms.

One of the greatest spiritual dangers is the temptation to conform to the values and practices of the world. Romans 12:2 again warns, "Do not be conformed to this world, but be transformed by the renewal of your mind." The world's values often stand in direct opposition to God's truth, and conforming to them can lead us away from God's will.

Materialism is another significant source of spiritual disease. In a world that often measures success and worth by material possessions, it is easy to fall into the trap of prioritizing wealth and comfort over spiritual growth. 1 Timothy 6:9-10 warns, "But those who desire to be rich fall into temptation, into a snare, into many senseless and harmful desires that plunge people into ruin and destruction. For the love of money is a root of all kinds of evils." Guarding against materialism requires a conscious effort to focus on eternal values rather than temporary wealth.

The influence of secular media and entertainment is another potential source of spiritual disease. Many forms of media promote values and behaviors that are contrary to God's Word, and exposure to these influences can subtly shape our thoughts and attitudes. Psalm 101:3 declares, "I will not set before my eyes anything that is worthless. I hate the work of those who fall away; it shall not cling to me." By being selective about what we watch, read, and listen to, we can protect our minds and hearts from being corrupted.

Additionally, the pressure to conform to societal norms can lead to spiritual compromise. Whether it is the pressure to accept unbiblical beliefs, engage in immoral behaviors, or adopt a lifestyle that is contrary to God's Word, societal pressure can be a powerful force that leads us away from God. Acts 5:29 offers a clear response to such pressure: "But Peter and the apostles answered, 'We must obey God rather than men.'" Maintaining our commitment to God's truth, even in the face of societal opposition, is essential for safeguarding our spiritual health.

How Can You Safeguard Your Mind and Heart?

Safeguarding your mind and heart requires a proactive and intentional approach to spiritual health. One of the most effective ways to protect yourself is to immerse yourself in God's Word. Psalm 119:11 again emphasizes the importance of Scripture: "I have stored up your word in my heart, that I might not sin against you." By regularly reading, studying, and meditating on the Bible, you fill your mind and heart with God's truth, which acts as a shield against spiritual attacks.

Prayer is another essential safeguard. Ephesians 6:18 encourages believers to pray "at all times in the Spirit, with all prayer and supplication." Through prayer, we maintain our connection with God, seek His guidance, and receive His strength to resist temptation and stand firm in our faith.

In addition to Scripture and prayer, fellowship with other believers is crucial for safeguarding your mind and heart. Hebrews 10:24-25 again exhorts, "And let us consider how to stir up one another to love and good works, not neglecting to meet together, as is the habit of some, but encouraging one another, and all the more as you see the Day drawing near." Being part of a Christian community provides accountability, encouragement, and support as you navigate the challenges of the spiritual life.

Another important safeguard is to cultivate a lifestyle of worship. Worship is not just an activity reserved for church services but a way of life that honors God in all things. Colossians 3:16 again encourages, "Let the word of Christ dwell in you richly, teaching and admonishing one another in all wisdom, singing psalms and hymns and spiritual songs, with thankfulness in your hearts to God." A heart that is continually focused on worshiping God is less likely to be swayed by the distractions and temptations of the world.

Finally, practicing regular self-examination and repentance helps keep your mind and heart aligned with God's will. 2 Corinthians 13:5 again advises, "Examine yourselves, to see whether you are in the faith. Test yourselves. Or do you not realize this about yourselves, that Jesus Christ is in you?—unless indeed you fail to meet the test!" By regularly reflecting on your spiritual condition and seeking God's help to address any areas of concern, you can prevent spiritual sickness from taking root.

Spiritual Health Leads to Eternal Life— Keep Your Eye on the Prize

Maintaining spiritual health is not just about avoiding sickness— it is about pursuing the abundant life that God promises to those who follow Him. Jesus said in John 10:10, "The thief comes only to steal and kill and destroy. I came that they may have life and have it abundantly." This abundant life is characterized by a deep and growing relationship with God, marked by joy, peace, and fulfillment.

However, the ultimate goal of spiritual health is not just a better life here on earth but eternal life with God. Paul writes in Philippians 3:13-14, "Brothers, I do not consider that I have made it my own. But one thing I do: forgetting what lies behind and straining forward to what lies ahead, I press on toward the goal for the prize of the upward call of God in Christ Jesus." Keeping our eyes on the prize of eternal life motivates us to maintain our spiritual health and remain faithful in our walk with God.

In 2 Timothy 4:7-8, Paul reflects on his own journey, saying, "I have fought the good fight, I have finished the race, I have kept the faith. Henceforth there is laid up for me the crown of righteousness, which the Lord, the righteous judge, will award to me on that Day, and not only to me but also to all who have loved his appearing." This crown of righteousness represents the reward for those who have remained spiritually healthy and faithful to the end.

To keep our eye on the prize, we must remain vigilant and committed to our spiritual growth. Hebrews 12:1-2 again encourages us, "Therefore, since we are surrounded by so great a cloud of witnesses, let us also lay aside every weight, and sin which clings so closely, and let us run with endurance the race that is set before us, looking to Jesus, the founder and perfecter of our faith, who for the joy that was set before him endured the cross, despising the shame, and is seated at the right hand of the throne of God." By focusing on Jesus and the eternal rewards that await us, we can persevere in our pursuit of spiritual health and ultimately receive the crown of life that God has promised.

CHAPTER 9 How Can We Develop the Right Desires?

Choose Life: Aligning Desires with God's Will

In developing the right desires, the first step is to align our desires with the will of God. This requires a conscious choice to "choose life," as Moses urged the Israelites in Deuteronomy 30:19: "I call heaven and earth to witness against you today, that I have set before you life and death, blessing and curse. Therefore, choose life, that you and your offspring may live." Choosing life means prioritizing God's will and purpose over our own natural inclinations, which are often influenced by the world and the flesh.

The natural human heart is inclined towards sin and self-interest, as Jeremiah 17:9 warns, "The heart is deceitful above all things, and desperately sick; who can understand it?" Therefore, to develop the right desires, we must first acknowledge the flawed state of our hearts and seek God's transformation through His Word and Spirit.

Developing the right desires involves a shift from self-centeredness to God-centeredness. This is not a one-time decision but an ongoing process of daily choosing to follow God's ways. Joshua 24:15 exemplifies this choice: "And if it is evil in your eyes to serve Jehovah, choose this day whom you will serve, whether the gods your fathers served in the region beyond the River, or the gods of the Amorites in whose land you dwell. But as for me and my house, we will serve Jehovah." Like Joshua, we must commit to serving God and pursuing His desires above all else.

This choice to align our desires with God's will requires us to continually assess and evaluate our motivations and intentions. Psalm 139:23-24 is a prayer that encapsulates this need for introspection: "Search me, O God, and know my heart! Try me and know my thoughts! And see if there be any grievous way in me, and lead me in the way everlasting!" By regularly seeking God's examination of our hearts, we can identify and root out desires that are contrary to His will.

Desire the Pure Spiritual Milk: Nourishing Godly Desires

Developing the right desires also requires us to nourish our spiritual lives with the "pure spiritual milk" of God's Word. 1 Peter 2:2-3 encourages believers, "Like newborn infants, long for the pure spiritual milk, that by it you may grow up into salvation—if indeed you have tasted that Jehovah is good." Just as physical growth depends on proper nourishment, spiritual growth depends on feeding our minds and hearts with God's truth.

The desire for God's Word is foundational to developing the right desires because it is through Scripture that we learn about God's character, His promises, and His will for our lives. Psalm 119:11 underscores the importance of internalizing God's Word: "I have stored up your word in my heart, that I might not sin against you." By storing God's Word in our hearts, we equip ourselves to resist sinful desires and cultivate desires that align with His will.

Furthermore, the pure spiritual milk of God's Word not only informs our desires but also transforms them. Hebrews 4:12 again describes the transformative power of Scripture: "For the word of God is living and active, sharper than any two-edged sword, piercing to the division of soul and of spirit, of joints and of marrow, and discerning the thoughts and intentions of the heart." As we immerse ourselves in Scripture, God's Word works within us to reshape our desires, making them more like His.

Nourishing godly desires also involves surrounding ourselves with influences that reinforce our commitment to God's will. Proverbs 13:20 advises, "Whoever walks with the wise becomes wise, but the companion of fools will suffer harm." By choosing to associate with others who share our commitment to God's Word, we strengthen our own resolve to pursue godly desires.

For As He Thinks in His Heart, So Is He: The Power of Thought in Shaping Desires

The development of right desires is deeply connected to the thoughts that occupy our minds. Proverbs 23:7 (UASV) states, "For as he thinks in his heart, so is he." This verse highlights the profound truth that our thoughts shape our identity and, by extension, our desires. Therefore, to develop the right desires, we must first cultivate right thinking.

Right thinking begins with a conscious decision to reject thoughts that are contrary to God's will and to focus instead on what is true, honorable, just, pure, lovely, and commendable, as instructed in Philippians 4:8. The apostle Paul further emphasizes the importance of setting our minds on things above rather than on earthly things in Colossians 3:2: "Set your minds on things that are above, not on things that are on earth." By directing our thoughts towards God and His kingdom, we align our desires with His purposes.

However, controlling our thoughts is not always easy, especially in a world filled with distractions and temptations. 2 Corinthians 10:5 again exhorts us to "take every thought captive to obey Christ." This means being vigilant about what we allow into our minds and actively filtering out thoughts that do not align with God's truth. Whether it is through prayer, meditation on Scripture, or the encouragement of fellow believers, taking our thoughts captive is essential for developing desires that honor God.

In addition to guarding our thoughts, we must also be intentional about what we feed our minds. Romans 12:2 again reminds us of the need for mental renewal: "Do not be conformed to this world, but be transformed by the renewal of your mind, that by testing you may discern what is the will of God, what is good and acceptable and perfect." Renewing our minds through Scripture, prayer, and worship helps us develop the right desires and equips us to resist the influence of worldly desires.

Do Not Love the World: Overcoming Worldly Desires

One of the greatest challenges in developing the right desires is overcoming the allure of worldly desires. 1 John 2:15-17 again warns believers, "Do not love the world or the things in the world. If anyone loves the world, the love of the Father is not in him. For all that is in the world—the desires of the flesh and the desires of the eyes and pride of life—is not from the Father but is from the world. And the world is passing away along with its desires, but whoever does the will of God abides forever." The love of the world is incompatible with the love of God, and worldly desires often lead us away from the path of righteousness.

To overcome worldly desires, we must first recognize their fleeting nature. The things of this world—wealth, power, fame, and pleasure—are temporary and ultimately unsatisfying. Ecclesiastes 5:10 reflects on the futility of pursuing wealth: "He who loves money will not be satisfied with money, nor he who loves wealth with his income; this also is vanity." By understanding the temporary and deceptive nature of worldly desires, we can begin to shift our focus to eternal values that bring true fulfillment.

Overcoming worldly desires also involves cultivating a deep and abiding love for God. When our love for God surpasses our love for the world, we find it easier to resist the temptations that the world offers. James 4:4 again starkly contrasts friendship with the world and friendship with God: "You adulterous people! Do you not know that friendship with the world is enmity with God? Therefore whoever wishes to be a friend of the world makes himself an enemy of God." By prioritizing our relationship with God and seeking to please Him above all else, we weaken the hold that worldly desires have on our hearts.

Another key to overcoming worldly desires is practicing contentment. 1 Timothy 6:6-8 again teaches, "But godliness with contentment is great gain, for we brought nothing into the world, and we cannot take anything out of the world. But if we have food and clothing, with these we will be content." Contentment frees us from the constant striving for more that characterizes worldly desires and helps us find satisfaction in the simple blessings that God provides.

The Spirit Versus the Flesh: The Internal Battle for Desires

The development of right desires is often described in Scripture as a battle between the Spirit and the flesh. Galatians 5:16-17 vividly describes this struggle: "But I say, walk by the Spirit, and you will not gratify the desires of the flesh. For the desires of the flesh are against the Spirit, and the desires of the Spirit are against the flesh, for these are opposed to each other, to keep you from doing the things you want to do." This internal conflict is a reality for every believer, as the sinful nature, or the flesh, constantly pulls us towards desires that are contrary to God's will.

The key to winning this battle lies in submitting to the Holy Spirit's leading. Romans 8:5-6 again explains, "For those who live according to the flesh set their minds on the things of the flesh, but those who live according to the Spirit set their minds on the things of the Spirit. For to set the mind on the flesh is death, but to set the mind on the Spirit is life and peace." By setting our minds on the things of the Spirit, we align our desires with God's will and find the strength to resist the temptations of the flesh.

Walking by the Spirit also involves actively rejecting the works of the flesh, which are listed in Galatians 5:19-21: "Now the works of the flesh are evident: sexual immorality, impurity, sensuality, idolatry, sorcery, enmity, strife, jealousy, fits of anger, rivalries, dissensions, divisions, envy, drunkenness, orgies, and things like these." These sinful behaviors are rooted in desires that are opposed to God's will, and they must be put to death in our lives if we are to develop the right desires.

In contrast, the fruit of the Spirit, as described in Galatians 5:22-23, represents the desires and behaviors that align with God's will: "But the fruit of the Spirit is love, joy, peace, patience, kindness, goodness, faithfulness, gentleness, self-control; against such things there is no law." As we cultivate these fruits in our lives, we develop desires that reflect God's character and bring glory to Him.

To walk by the Spirit and overcome the desires of the flesh, we must also engage in regular self-discipline. 1 Corinthians 9:27 again illustrates the importance of self-control in the Christian life: "But I discipline my body and keep it under control, lest after preaching to others I myself should be disqualified." Self-discipline helps us to resist the pull of the flesh and to stay focused on pursuing desires that honor God.

Bringing This Transformation About: Practical Steps to Developing the Right Desires

Developing the right desires requires intentional and practical steps that involve both the mind and the heart. One of the most effective ways to bring about this transformation is through regular and focused prayer. In Psalm 37:4, we are encouraged to "Delight yourself in Jehovah, and he will give you the desires of your heart." This verse is not a promise that God will fulfill every selfish desire but that as we delight in Him, our desires will increasingly align with His will. Prayer is the means by which we express our desires to God and invite Him to shape them according to His purposes.

Another practical step is to immerse ourselves in God's Word. Psalm 1:2-3 describes the blessedness of the one whose "delight is in the law of Jehovah, and on his law he meditates day and night. He is like a tree planted by streams of water that yields its fruit in its season, and its leaf does not wither. In all that he does, he prospers." Regular meditation on Scripture nourishes our souls and strengthens our resolve to pursue godly desires.

Accountability is also an essential component of developing the right desires. Proverbs 27:17 states, "Iron sharpens iron, and one man sharpens another." By seeking out the support and encouragement of fellow believers, we can hold each other accountable to pursuing desires that align with God's will.

In addition, we must be vigilant about guarding our hearts and minds against influences that could lead us astray. Proverbs 4:23 again advises, "Keep your heart with all vigilance, for from it flow the springs of life." This involves being selective about the media we consume, the conversations we engage in, and the environments we expose ourselves to.

Finally, cultivating gratitude is a powerful way to develop the right desires. 1 Thessalonians 5:18 again instructs, "Give thanks in all circumstances; for this is the will of God in Christ Jesus for you." Gratitude shifts our focus from what we lack to what God has already provided, fostering contentment and reducing the power of worldly desires.

The Old and the New Person: Putting Off the Old and Putting On the New

Developing the right desires is closely linked to the biblical concept of putting off the old person and putting on the new. Ephesians 4:22-24 again urges believers, "To put off your old self, which belongs to your former manner of life and is corrupt through deceitful desires, and to be renewed in the spirit of your minds, and to put on the new self, created after the likeness of God in true righteousness and holiness." This process of transformation involves a deliberate decision to reject the sinful desires of the old self and to embrace the desires of the new self, which is being renewed in the image of Christ.

Putting off the old self requires a conscious rejection of the habits, attitudes, and desires that characterized our life before Christ. Colossians 3:5-10 again provides a clear list of what must be put off: "Put to death therefore what is earthly in you: sexual immorality, impurity, passion, evil desire, and covetousness, which is idolatry. On account of these the wrath of God is coming. In these you too once walked, when you were living in them. But now you must put them all away: anger, wrath, malice, slander, and obscene talk from your mouth. Do not lie to one another, seeing that you have put off the old self with its practices and have put on the new self, which is being renewed in knowledge after the image of its creator."

Putting on the new self, on the other hand, involves embracing the desires and behaviors that reflect the character of Christ. Colossians 3:12-14 again instructs, "Put on then, as God's chosen ones, holy and beloved, compassionate hearts, kindness, humility, meekness, and patience, bearing with one another and, if one has a complaint against another, forgiving each other; as Jehovah has forgiven you, so you also must forgive. And above all these put on love, which binds everything together in perfect harmony." The new self is marked by virtues that promote unity, love, and godliness, and it is through the development of these virtues that we cultivate the right desires.

Maintain the Renewed Mind: The Ongoing Process of Desire Transformation

The process of developing the right desires is ongoing and requires the continual renewal of our minds. Romans 12:2 again reminds us of the importance of mental renewal: "Do not be conformed to this world, but be transformed by the renewal of your mind, that by testing you may discern what is the will of God, what is good and acceptable and perfect." Renewing our minds involves consistently immersing ourselves in God's Word, prayer, and worship, allowing these spiritual disciplines to shape our thoughts and desires.

Maintaining a renewed mind also requires vigilance in guarding against influences that could corrupt our thinking. 1 Peter 5:8 again warns, "Be sober-minded; be watchful. Your adversary the devil prowls around like a roaring lion, seeking someone to devour." By staying alert to the enemy's tactics and resisting the temptations of the flesh, we protect our minds from being led astray.

In addition to guarding our minds, we must also actively pursue godly thinking. Philippians 4:8 again offers a blueprint for right thinking: "Finally, brothers, whatever is true, whatever is honorable, whatever is just, whatever is pure, whatever is lovely, whatever is commendable, if there is any excellence, if there is anything worthy of praise, think about these things." By filling our minds with thoughts that align with God's character, we strengthen our ability to develop and maintain the right desires.

Renewed Thinking: The Foundation for Right Desires

Renewed thinking is the foundation upon which right desires are built. Without the renewal of the mind, our desires will remain rooted in the flesh and the world. Ephesians 4:23-24 again emphasizes the connection between renewed thinking and the new self: "And to be renewed in the spirit of your minds, and to put on the new self, created after the likeness of God in true righteousness and holiness." As our thinking is renewed by God's truth, our desires are transformed to reflect His will.

Renewed thinking involves more than just intellectual assent to biblical truths; it requires a deep, heart-level transformation that affects every aspect of our lives. 2 Corinthians 5:17 again declares, "Therefore, if anyone is in Christ, he is a new creation. The old has passed away; behold, the new has come." This new creation involves a complete overhaul of our desires, motivations, and priorities, aligning them with God's purposes.

One practical way to cultivate renewed thinking is through the practice of biblical meditation. Joshua 1:8 again instructs, "This Book of the Law shall not depart from your mouth, but you shall meditate on it day and night, so that you may be careful to do according to all that is written in it. For then you will make your way prosperous, and then you will have good success." Meditation on Scripture allows God's Word to penetrate our minds and hearts, renewing our thinking and shaping our desires.

Even Still the Battle Wages On: The Ongoing Struggle to Develop Right Desires

While we are called to develop right desires, the reality is that the battle against sinful desires is ongoing. Galatians 5:17 again reminds us, "For the desires of the flesh are against the Spirit, and the desires of the Spirit are against the flesh, for these are opposed to each other, to keep you from doing the things you want to do." This internal conflict is a part of the Christian life, and it requires perseverance and reliance on God's strength.

In Romans 7:21-23, Paul again describes his own struggle with sinful desires: "So I find it to be a law that when I want to do right, evil lies close at hand. For I delight in the law of God, in my inner being, but I see in my members another law waging war against the law of my mind and making me captive to the law of sin that dwells in my members." Paul's honesty about his struggle serves as an encouragement to us that we are not alone in this battle and that victory is possible through Christ.

The key to victory in this ongoing battle is to rely on the power of the Holy Spirit. Romans 8:13 again offers this assurance: "For if you live according to the flesh you will die, but if by the Spirit you put to death the deeds of the body, you will live." The Holy Spirit empowers us to resist sinful desires and to cultivate desires that honor God.

The Relativity of Your Christian Freedom: Balancing Freedom and Responsibility in Desire Development

As believers, we have been given freedom in Christ, but this freedom comes with the responsibility to use it in a way that honors God and serves others. Galatians 5:13 again instructs, "For you were called to freedom, brothers. Only do not use your freedom as an opportunity for the flesh, but through love serve one another." The freedom we have in Christ is not a license to indulge sinful desires but an opportunity to develop desires that reflect God's love and righteousness.

Balancing freedom and responsibility in desire development requires discernment and wisdom. 1 Corinthians 6:12 again highlights the importance of exercising our freedom with care: "All things are lawful for me, but not all things are helpful. All things are lawful for me, but I will not be dominated by anything." While we have the freedom to make choices, we must consider whether those choices are beneficial and whether they lead us closer to God or away from Him.

In addition to exercising discernment, we must also be mindful of how our desires and actions affect others. Romans 14:13 again cautions, "Therefore let us not pass judgment on one another any longer, but rather decide never to put a stumbling block or hindrance in the way of a brother." Our freedom should never be used in a way that causes others to stumble or weakens their faith.

Ultimately, the goal of our Christian freedom is to glorify God in all that we do. 1 Corinthians 10:31 again declares, "So, whether you eat or drink, or whatever you do, do all to the glory of God." By using our freedom to pursue desires that honor God and serve others, we fulfill the purpose for which we were created.

CHAPTER 10 How Can We Cope with Life's Problems Through God's Guidance?

What Reasons Have We for Optimism as to Life's Problems? How Is God Involved?

Life's problems, whether they be personal struggles, relational conflicts, or global crises, can often seem overwhelming. However, as Christians, we have profound reasons for optimism, rooted in our faith and trust in Jehovah God. The Bible offers us assurance that Jehovah is deeply involved in our lives, providing guidance, support, and comfort as we navigate through our challenges.

One of the primary reasons for optimism is the knowledge that Jehovah cares for us and is aware of our struggles. 1 Peter 5:7 encourages us to "cast all your anxieties on him, because he cares for you." This verse assures us that we are not alone in our difficulties; Jehovah is with us, ready to help us bear our burdens. His involvement in our lives is not distant or detached, but personal and intimate. As our loving Father, He is deeply concerned with our well-being and actively works for our good.

Moreover, we have the promise of Jehovah's presence and guidance in every situation. Isaiah 41:10 offers a powerful reassurance: "Fear not, for I am with you; be not dismayed, for I am your God; I will strengthen you, I will help you, I will uphold you with my righteous right hand." This verse emphasizes Jehovah's commitment to us, promising that He will strengthen and uphold us, no matter the circumstances we face. Knowing that Jehovah is with us gives us the confidence to face life's problems with hope and courage.

Another reason for optimism is the understanding that Jehovah uses life's difficulties to refine and strengthen our faith. James 1:2-4 encourages believers to "count it all joy, my brothers, when you meet trials of various kinds, for you know that the testing of your faith produces steadfastness. And let steadfastness have its full effect, that you may be perfect and complete, lacking in nothing." While trials are never easy, they are opportunities for spiritual growth and maturity. Jehovah allows these challenges to develop our character, deepen our dependence on Him, and strengthen our faith.

Jehovah's involvement in our lives also includes His provision of peace and comfort, even in the midst of turmoil. Philippians 4:6-7 again instructs, "Do not be anxious about anything, but in everything by prayer and supplication with thanksgiving let your requests be made known to God. And the peace of God, which surpasses all understanding, will guard your hearts and your minds in Christ Jesus." When we bring our concerns to Jehovah in prayer, He promises to give us His peace—a peace that transcends human understanding and guards our hearts and minds from anxiety.

Finally, we have the ultimate reason for optimism: the hope of eternal life. Titus 1:2 speaks of the "hope of eternal life, which God, who never lies, promised before the ages began." This hope gives us a long-term perspective, reminding us that our present sufferings are temporary and that we have the promise of eternal life with Jehovah in the new heaven and new earth. This hope sustains us through life's challenges, giving us the strength to persevere and remain faithful.

How Severe Is the Problem of Stress?

Stress is one of the most pervasive problems in modern life, affecting people of all ages and backgrounds. It can arise from a variety of sources, including work-related pressures, financial difficulties, family conflicts, and health concerns. The effects of stress can be profound, impacting not only our mental and emotional well-being but also our physical health. Chronic stress has been linked to a range of health issues, including heart disease, high blood pressure, diabetes, and depression.

The severity of the problem of stress is compounded by the fact that it often goes unrecognized or unaddressed. Many people view stress as an inevitable part of life and may not seek help or take steps to manage it until it becomes overwhelming. Additionally, societal pressures to succeed, achieve, and maintain a certain lifestyle can contribute to a culture of stress, where individuals feel constantly under pressure to perform and meet expectations.

The Bible acknowledges the reality of stress and provides guidance on how to cope with it. Psalm 55:22 offers this counsel: "Cast your burden on Jehovah, and he will sustain you; he will never permit the righteous to be moved." This verse reminds us that we do not have to carry our burdens alone; we can cast them on Jehovah and trust that He will sustain us. By bringing our concerns to Jehovah in prayer, we can experience His sustaining power and find relief from the weight of stress.

Stress is also exacerbated by the uncertainty and unpredictability of life. Jesus acknowledged this reality in Matthew 6:34, saying, "Therefore do not be anxious about tomorrow, for tomorrow will be anxious for itself. Sufficient for the day is its own trouble." Jesus' words remind us that while we cannot control the future, we can trust in Jehovah's provision and care for each day. By focusing on the present and relying on Jehovah, we can reduce the stress that comes from worrying about the future.

Furthermore, stress can be alleviated by adopting a balanced perspective on life. Ecclesiastes 4:6 offers this wisdom: "Better is a handful of quietness than two hands full of toil and a striving after wind." This verse highlights the importance of contentment and simplicity, reminding us that the pursuit of material success and the constant striving for more can lead to stress and dissatisfaction. By prioritizing peace and contentment over the relentless pursuit of wealth and achievement, we can reduce the sources of stress in our lives.

How Can Bible Counsel Help Us to Cope with Stress?

The Bible offers practical and effective counsel for coping with stress, providing us with strategies to manage our emotions, find peace, and maintain a balanced perspective on life. One of the most powerful tools the Bible offers for coping with stress is prayer. Philippians 4:6-7 again encourages us to bring our anxieties to Jehovah in prayer: "Do not be anxious about anything, but in everything by prayer and supplication with thanksgiving let your requests be made known to God. And the peace of God, which surpasses all understanding, will guard your hearts and your minds in Christ Jesus." Prayer allows us to release our burdens to Jehovah, trusting that He will provide the peace and strength we need to cope with our challenges.

In addition to prayer, the Bible encourages us to practice gratitude as a way to cope with stress. 1 Thessalonians 5:18 again instructs, "Give thanks in all circumstances; for this is the will of God in Christ Jesus for you." Gratitude shifts our focus from what we lack or what is causing us stress to the blessings we have received from Jehovah. By cultivating an attitude of thankfulness, we can counteract the negative effects of stress and maintain a positive outlook on life.

Another important aspect of coping with stress is maintaining a balanced perspective. Jesus taught the importance of prioritizing spiritual matters over worldly concerns in Matthew 6:33: "But seek first the kingdom of God and his righteousness, and all these things will be added to you." When we focus on our relationship with Jehovah and seek His righteousness, we can trust that He will take care of our needs, reducing the stress that comes from worrying about material concerns.

The Bible also emphasizes the importance of rest and renewal as a way to cope with stress. Exodus 20:8-10 again instructs, "Remember the Sabbath day, to keep it holy. Six days you shall labor, and do all your work, but the seventh day is a Sabbath to Jehovah your God." While Christians are not under the Mosaic Law, the principle of rest remains valuable. Taking time to rest, reflect, and renew our spirits is essential for managing stress and maintaining our overall well-being.

Finally, the Bible encourages us to seek the support of others as we cope with stress. Ecclesiastes 4:9-10 again reminds us, "Two are better than one, because they have a good reward for their toil. For if they fall, one will lift up his fellow. But woe to him who is alone when he falls and has not another to lift him up!" Having a support network of family, friends, and fellow believers can provide the encouragement and help we need to navigate stressful situations. By leaning on others and allowing them to support us, we can share the burden of stress and find comfort in their companionship.

Scientists Have Found What About the Bible's Counsel on Love?

Modern scientific research has increasingly recognized the profound impact of love, compassion, and positive relationships on mental and physical health. Studies have shown that individuals who experience love and positive social connections tend to have lower levels of stress, anxiety, and depression, as well as better overall health outcomes. This aligns with the Bible's counsel on the importance of love and the positive effects it has on our well-being.

The Bible teaches that love is not only a fundamental commandment but also a powerful force for good in our lives. Jesus emphasized the centrality of love in Matthew 22:37-39: "And he said to him, 'You shall love Jehovah your God with all your heart and with all your soul and with all your mind. This is the great and first commandment. And a second is like it: You shall love your neighbor as yourself.'" These commandments highlight the importance of love for God and for others as the foundation of a healthy and fulfilling life.

Scientists have found that love and social support can have a protective effect on our health, reducing the harmful effects of stress and promoting resilience in the face of challenges. The Bible's counsel to love one another is not only a moral imperative but also a practical guide for maintaining mental and emotional health. John 13:34-35 again records Jesus' words: "A new commandment I give to you, that you love one another: just as I have loved you, you also are to love one another. By this all people will know that you are my disciples, if you have love for one another." Love fosters a sense of belonging and connection, which are essential for emotional well-being.

Furthermore, the Bible's counsel on forgiveness, another aspect of love, has been shown to have significant health benefits. Holding onto anger, bitterness, and resentment can contribute to stress, anxiety, and physical health problems. In contrast, forgiveness promotes healing and reduces the burden of negative emotions. Colossians 3:13

again exhorts believers, "Bearing with one another and, if one has a complaint against another, forgiving each other; as Jehovah has forgiven you, so you also must forgive." Forgiveness not only benefits the person who is forgiven but also brings peace and relief to the one who forgives.

In addition, the Bible's emphasis on love as a selfless, sacrificial act aligns with scientific findings on the benefits of altruism and helping others. Acts of kindness and service have been shown to increase feelings of happiness and satisfaction, reduce stress, and even improve physical health. Philippians 2:3-4 again encourages believers to adopt an attitude of selflessness: "Do nothing from selfish ambition or conceit, but in humility count others more significant than yourselves. Let each of you look not only to his own interests but also to the interests of others." By following the Bible's counsel to love and serve others, we not only obey God's commandments but also enhance our own well-being.

How Else Can the Bible's Counsel Help Us with Stress?

In addition to the principles of love, forgiveness, and selflessness, the Bible offers other practical counsel that can help us manage and reduce stress. One of these principles is the importance of living a life of integrity and honesty. Proverbs 10:9 again teaches, "Whoever walks in integrity walks securely, but he who makes his ways crooked will be found out." Living with integrity reduces the stress that comes from trying to cover up wrongdoing, maintain a false image, or deal with the consequences of dishonesty. When we live truthfully and uprightly, we experience the peace that comes from a clear conscience and the trust that others place in us.

The Bible also encourages us to cultivate humility, which can help alleviate stress by reducing the pressure to always be right, successful, or in control. 1 Peter 5:6-7 again advises, "Humble yourselves, therefore, under the mighty hand of God so that at the proper time he may exalt you, casting all your anxieties on him, because he cares for you." Humility allows us to acknowledge our limitations and depend on Jehovah's strength rather than our own. This reliance on God rather than on our own abilities relieves the stress of trying to carry the weight of the world on our shoulders.

Contentment is another biblical principle that can help us cope with stress. 1 Timothy 6:6-8 again states, "But godliness with contentment is great gain, for we brought nothing into the world, and we cannot take anything out of the world. But if we have food and clothing, with these we will be content." The pursuit of more—whether it be wealth, status, or possessions—can lead to chronic stress as we strive to meet ever-increasing demands and expectations. By cultivating contentment, we free ourselves from the stress of always wanting more and find peace in what Jehovah has provided.

The Bible also teaches the importance of trust in Jehovah as a remedy for stress. Proverbs 3:5-6 again instructs, "Trust in Jehovah with all your heart, and do not lean on your own understanding. In all your ways acknowledge him, and he will make straight your paths." Trusting in Jehovah means recognizing that He is in control and that He has a plan for our lives. When we trust in Jehovah's wisdom and guidance, we can let go of the anxiety that comes from trying to control every aspect of our lives.

Finally, the Bible emphasizes the value of rest and Sabbath-like rest. Jesus Himself modeled the importance of rest when He took time away from the crowds to pray and be alone with Jehovah. Mark 6:31 again records, "And he said to them, 'Come away by yourselves to a desolate place and rest a while.' For many were coming and going, and they had no leisure even to eat." Rest is not just physical but also spiritual and emotional. Taking time to rest, reflect, and renew our spirits is essential for coping with stress and maintaining our overall well-being.

How Serious a Problem Is Loneliness?

Loneliness is a serious and pervasive problem that affects people of all ages and backgrounds. It is not merely the absence of physical companionship but the deep feeling of being disconnected, isolated, or unloved. The impact of loneliness on mental, emotional, and physical health is profound. Studies have shown that chronic loneliness can lead to depression, anxiety, sleep disturbances, and even increased risk of heart disease and premature death.

PUT OFF THE OLD PERSON

The Bible acknowledges the reality of loneliness and provides comfort and counsel for those who experience it. Psalm 25:16 again reflects the psalmist's cry for connection: "Turn to me and be gracious to me, for I am lonely and afflicted." This verse reminds us that loneliness is a common human experience, but it is also an opportunity to turn to Jehovah and seek His comfort and presence.

Jehovah's presence is a powerful antidote to loneliness. Psalm 139:7-10 again assures us of Jehovah's constant presence: "Where shall I go from your Spirit? Or where shall I flee from your presence? If I ascend to heaven, you are there! If I make my bed in Sheol, you are there! If I take the wings of the morning and dwell in the uttermost parts of the sea, even there your hand shall lead me, and your right hand shall hold me." Knowing that Jehovah is always with us provides comfort and reassurance, even in our loneliest moments.

In addition to Jehovah's presence, the Bible encourages us to seek out and maintain relationships with others as a way to combat loneliness. Ecclesiastes 4:9-12 again highlights the importance of companionship: "Two are better than one, because they have a good reward for their toil. For if they fall, one will lift up his fellow. But woe to him who is alone when he falls and has not another to lift him up!" By fostering connections with family, friends, and fellow believers, we create a support network that helps to alleviate feelings of loneliness.

Christian fellowship is also a vital source of support and connection for those struggling with loneliness. Hebrews 10:24-25 again encourages believers to "consider how to stir up one another to love and good works, not neglecting to meet together, as is the habit of some, but encouraging one another, and all the more as you see the Day drawing near." Regular fellowship with other believers provides encouragement, accountability, and a sense of belonging, which are essential for overcoming loneliness.

Finally, the Bible calls us to reach out to others who may be experiencing loneliness. James 1:27 again defines true religion as "to visit orphans and widows in their affliction, and to keep oneself unstained from the world." By showing compassion and care for those who are lonely, we not only fulfill our Christian duty but also create meaningful connections that can alleviate our own feelings of isolation.

CHAPTER 11 How Can We Distinguish Right from Wrong in a World of Moral Confusion?

Our Power of Perception: Navigating the Popularity and Glamor of Wrongdoing

In a world increasingly influenced by the popularity and glamor of wrongdoing, the challenge of distinguishing right from wrong becomes ever more critical. The Bible warns against the deceptive allure of sin, which often presents itself as desirable and even glamorous. Proverbs 14:12 reminds us, "There is a way that seems right to a man, but its end is the way to death." This verse highlights the danger of relying on our own perceptions or the prevailing cultural norms to determine what is right.

The power of perception is a gift from God, enabling us to observe, analyze, and make judgments about the world around us. However, this power must be guided by divine wisdom, not by the shifting standards of society. Romans 12:2 instructs believers, "Do not be conformed to this world, but be transformed by the renewal of your mind, that by testing you may discern what is the will of God, what is good and acceptable and perfect." The renewal of our minds through God's Word is essential for sharpening our perception and enabling us to see through the deceptions of the world.

The popularity of wrongdoing is often bolstered by peer pressure, a powerful force that can sway even the strongest individuals. Exodus 23:2 warns, "You shall not follow a multitude to do evil, nor shall you bear witness in a lawsuit, siding with the many, so as to pervert justice." This commandment underscores the importance of resisting the influence of the majority, especially when it leads to compromising moral principles. Peer pressure can lead to the normalization of sin, making it appear acceptable or even virtuous. Therefore, believers must remain vigilant, recognizing that what is popular is not always right.

The glamorization of wrongdoing is another challenge to our moral discernment. Sin is often portrayed as exciting, liberating, or fulfilling, while righteousness is depicted as dull or restrictive. Isaiah 5:20 pronounces a woe on those who "call evil good and good evil, who put darkness for light and light for darkness, who put bitter for sweet and sweet for bitter!" This inversion of moral values is a hallmark of a society in moral decline, where the lines between right and wrong are deliberately blurred.

To navigate these challenges, we must anchor our perceptions in the unchanging truth of God's Word. Psalm 119:105 declares, "Your word is a lamp to my feet and a light to my path." Scripture provides the clarity and guidance we need to see through the distortions of the world and to walk in the light of God's truth.

Right and Wrong: What Guides Many?

In determining what is right and wrong, many people rely on three common but unreliable guides: their feelings, the opinions of others, and the desire to fit in. While these guides may seem reasonable, they are often influenced by subjective, temporary, and fallible factors, leading to moral confusion and compromise.

Our Feelings: Many people base their moral decisions on their emotions, believing that if something feels right, it must be right. However, the Bible warns against the unreliability of human emotions. Jeremiah 17:9 reveals, "The heart is deceitful above all things, and desperately sick; who can understand it?" Our feelings can be easily swayed by external circumstances, personal desires, or the influence of others, making them a poor guide for moral decisions. Proverbs 28:26 further cautions, "Whoever trusts in his own mind is a fool, but he who walks in wisdom will be delivered." Wisdom, which comes from God, must guide our decisions rather than our fluctuating emotions.

What Other People Think: The opinions of others, especially those of influential or admired individuals, can significantly impact our sense of right and wrong. Social media, entertainment, and popular culture often shape public opinion, promoting certain behaviors as acceptable or desirable. However, the Bible reminds us that the approval of others is not a reliable measure of morality. Galatians 1:10 challenges us, "For am I now seeking the approval of man, or of God? Or am I trying to please man? If I were still trying to please man, I would not be a servant of Christ." Our primary concern should be pleasing God, not conforming to the opinions of others.

Wanting to Fit In: The desire to fit in and be accepted by our peers can lead us to compromise our moral principles. This is especially true in situations where standing up for what is right may result in rejection, ridicule, or persecution. However, the Bible calls us to stand firm in our convictions, even when it is unpopular or difficult. Matthew 5:10-12 offers encouragement, "Blessed are those who are persecuted for righteousness' sake, for theirs is the kingdom of heaven. Blessed are you when others revile you and persecute you and utter all kinds of evil against you falsely on my account. Rejoice and be glad, for your reward is great in heaven, for so they persecuted the prophets who were before you." Our desire to fit in must never override our commitment to righteousness.

The Better Guide: The Bible

In contrast to the unreliable guides of feelings, public opinion, and peer pressure, the Bible stands as the ultimate and unchanging guide for distinguishing right from wrong. 2 Timothy 3:16-17 affirms, "All Scripture is breathed out by God and profitable for teaching, for reproof, for correction, and for training in righteousness, that the man of God may be complete, equipped for every good work." The Bible is not just a collection of moral teachings; it is the inspired Word of God, providing the wisdom and guidance we need to live a life that is pleasing to Him.

The Bible's moral teachings are rooted in the character of God, who is holy, just, and loving. Psalm 19:7-9 again describes the perfection of God's law: "The law of Jehovah is perfect, reviving the soul; the testimony of Jehovah is sure, making wise the simple; the precepts of Jehovah are right, rejoicing the heart; the commandment of Jehovah is pure, enlightening the eyes; the fear of Jehovah is clean, enduring forever; the rules of Jehovah are true, and righteous altogether." God's law is not arbitrary but reflects His nature and His will for humanity. By following the Bible's teachings, we align ourselves with God's righteousness and wisdom.

The Bible also provides specific commands and principles that address a wide range of moral issues, from honesty and integrity to justice and mercy. These teachings are not just for individual conduct but also for how we interact with others and how we contribute to society. Micah 6:8 again summarizes the essence of biblical morality: "He has told you, O man, what is good; and what does Jehovah require of you but to do justice, and to love kindness, and to walk humbly with your God?" This verse encapsulates the moral vision of the Bible, calling us to live in a way that reflects God's justice, kindness, and humility.

In addition to providing moral guidance, the Bible also equips us to discern and resist the deceptions of the world. Hebrews 4:12 describes the Word of God as "living and active, sharper than any two-edged sword, piercing to the division of soul and of spirit, of joints and of marrow, and discerning the thoughts and intentions of the heart." The Bible helps us to see through the falsehoods and half-truths that often characterize worldly wisdom, enabling us to stand firm in the truth.

Can You Trust Your Own Judgment?

While human judgment is a valuable tool, it is also limited and fallible. Proverbs 3:5-7 again offers a sobering reminder: "Trust in Jehovah with all your heart, and do not lean on your own understanding. In all your ways acknowledge him, and he will make straight your paths. Be not wise in your own eyes; fear Jehovah, and turn away from evil." These verses caution us against overestimating our own wisdom and understanding, urging us instead to rely on Jehovah's guidance.

The limitations of human judgment are evident in the way people often justify their actions, even when those actions are clearly wrong. Proverbs 16:2 observes, "All the ways of a man are pure in his own eyes, but Jehovah weighs the spirit." This verse highlights the tendency of people to rationalize their behavior, often convincing themselves that their actions are justified or even virtuous. However, Jehovah sees beyond our self-justifications and judges the true motives of our hearts.

The Bible also warns against the dangers of pride, which can cloud our judgment and lead us astray. Proverbs 16:18 again states, "Pride goes before destruction, and a haughty spirit before a fall." Pride can make us resistant to correction, unwilling to admit our mistakes, and eager to assert our own opinions over the wisdom of others. In contrast, humility allows us to recognize our limitations and to seek God's guidance in making decisions.

To ensure that our judgment is trustworthy, we must constantly evaluate it in light of Scripture. James 1:22-25 again exhorts us, "But be doers of the word, and not hearers only, deceiving yourselves. For if anyone is a hearer of the word and not a doer, he is like a man who looks intently at his natural face in a mirror. For he looks at himself and goes away and at once forgets what he was like. But the one who looks into the perfect law, the law of liberty, and perseveres, being no hearer who forgets but a doer who acts, he will be blessed in his doing." By aligning our actions with the teachings of Scripture, we ensure that our judgment is grounded in God's truth rather than in our own flawed reasoning.

Finding the Strength to Do Good

Even when we know what is right, doing it can be challenging. The Bible acknowledges the struggle between the desire to do good and the pull of sin. Romans 7:18-19 again expresses this internal conflict: "For I know that nothing good dwells in me, that is, in my flesh. For I have the desire to do what is right, but not the ability to carry it out. For I do not do the good I want, but the evil I do not want is what I keep on doing." This passage reflects the reality that even the most committed believers can struggle to live out their convictions.

PUT OFF THE OLD PERSON

The strength to do good comes not from our own willpower but from God's grace and the empowering presence of the Holy Spirit. Philippians 2:13 again encourages believers with this truth: "For it is God who works in you, both to will and to work for his good pleasure." God is actively at work in us, giving us both the desire and the ability to do what is right. This divine assistance is essential for overcoming the weaknesses of our flesh and living a life that pleases God.

In addition to God's grace, we find strength to do good through prayer. Jesus taught the importance of prayer in resisting temptation and doing God's will in Matthew 26:41: "Watch and pray that you may not enter into temptation. The spirit indeed is willing, but the flesh is weak." Prayer connects us to God's power, enabling us to overcome the temptations and challenges that we face. By regularly seeking God's help in prayer, we cultivate the spiritual strength needed to live according to His will.

Fellowship with other believers is another source of strength in doing good. Hebrews 10:24-25 again advises, "And let us consider how to stir up one another to love and good works, not neglecting to meet together, as is the habit of some, but encouraging one another, and all the more as you see the Day drawing near." The support and encouragement of fellow Christians can inspire us to persevere in doing good, even when it is difficult or unpopular. By participating in a community of faith, we are strengthened in our resolve to live out our convictions.

Finally, the example of Jesus provides both the model and the motivation for doing good. 1 Peter 2:21 again reminds us, "For to this you have been called, because Christ also suffered for you, leaving you an example, so that you might follow in his steps." Jesus' life was characterized by selfless service, love, and obedience to God's will, even in the face of suffering. As we follow His example, we find the strength and inspiration to do good, knowing that we are walking in the path He has set before us.

CHAPTER 12 How Can We Walk in Integrity and Uphold Moral Standards in Every Aspect of Our Lives?

What Is Integrity?

Integrity is a quality that is often spoken of but not always fully understood or consistently practiced. In its simplest form, integrity refers to the consistency of one's actions, thoughts, and words with a set of moral and ethical principles. It is the state of being whole, undivided, and incorruptible. Biblically, integrity is closely tied to righteousness and the fear of Jehovah, as it reflects a commitment to living according to God's standards in every aspect of life.

The Hebrew word for integrity, "tom" or "tummah," conveys the idea of completeness, blamelessness, and moral purity. Proverbs 10:9 declares, "Whoever walks in integrity walks securely, but he who makes his ways crooked will be found out." This verse highlights the protective nature of integrity, as it provides a secure foundation for life. A person of integrity is not easily shaken or led astray because their life is built on the solid rock of God's truth.

Integrity is not merely about external behavior; it begins in the heart. Psalm 51:6 again states, "Behold, you delight in truth in the inward being, and you teach me wisdom in the secret heart." Jehovah desires truth and sincerity in our innermost being, not just outward compliance with His commands. Integrity involves aligning our inner thoughts and motives with God's will, ensuring that there is no hypocrisy or duplicity in our lives.

Moreover, integrity is a reflection of God's character. Psalm 25:21 again expresses a desire for divine guidance in maintaining integrity: "May integrity and uprightness preserve me, for I wait for you."

Jehovah Himself is described as a God of truth and righteousness, and He calls His people to mirror these qualities in their lives. When we walk in integrity, we are living in a way that honors God and reflects His holiness to the world.

What If You Do Not Keep Your Integrity?

Failing to keep one's integrity can have serious spiritual and relational consequences. Integrity is foundational to trust and credibility, and when it is compromised, the damage can be extensive. Proverbs 11:3 again warns, "The integrity of the upright guides them, but the crookedness of the treacherous destroys them." This verse illustrates the contrast between the guidance that integrity provides and the destruction that follows when integrity is abandoned.

When a person fails to maintain integrity, they not only harm their own soul but also undermine their witness as a follower of Christ. Matthew 5:13 again uses the metaphor of salt to describe the influence of believers: "You are the salt of the earth, but if salt has lost its taste, how shall its saltiness be restored? It is no longer good for anything except to be thrown out and trampled under people's feet." Just as salt that has lost its flavor is worthless, so too is a Christian who has compromised their integrity. Their ability to influence others for good is diminished, and their testimony is called into question.

Furthermore, a lack of integrity leads to a divided heart, where one is torn between the ways of the world and the ways of God. James 1:8 again describes such a person as "a double-minded man, unstable in all his ways." This instability results from trying to serve two masters, which is ultimately impossible. Jesus Himself stated in Matthew 6:24, "No one can serve two masters, for either he will hate the one and love the other, or he will be devoted to the one and despise the other. You cannot serve God and money." Integrity requires an undivided commitment to Jehovah, where our allegiance is solely to Him and His kingdom.

The loss of integrity also leads to a loss of peace. Isaiah 48:22 again declares, "There is no peace," says Jehovah, "for the wicked." When we live in a way that is inconsistent with God's standards, our conscience is troubled, and we experience inner turmoil. This lack of peace is a warning sign that we have strayed from the path of righteousness and need to return to Jehovah with a repentant heart.

However, it is important to remember that Jehovah is merciful and willing to forgive those who genuinely repent and seek to restore their integrity. Psalm 51:10 again offers a prayer for restoration: "Create in me a clean heart, O God, and renew a right spirit within me." No matter how far we may have strayed, Jehovah's grace is sufficient to cleanse us and help us rebuild our lives on the foundation of integrity.

How Can You Be a Person of Integrity?

Becoming a person of integrity requires intentional effort and reliance on Jehovah's guidance. It is not something that happens by accident; rather, it is the result of daily choices to live according to God's Word. Psalm 119:9 again asks, "How can a young man keep his way pure? By guarding it according to your word." This verse underscores the importance of immersing ourselves in Scripture and allowing it to shape our thoughts, actions, and decisions.

To be a person of integrity, one must first have a deep and abiding relationship with Jehovah. Proverbs 3:5-6 again advises, "Trust in Jehovah with all your heart, and do not lean on your own understanding. In all your ways acknowledge him, and he will make straight your paths." Trusting in Jehovah means relying on His wisdom and guidance rather than our own limited understanding. It involves seeking His will in all aspects of life and being willing to submit to His authority.

Integrity also requires a commitment to truthfulness. Ephesians 4:25 again exhorts, "Therefore, having put away falsehood, let each one of you speak the truth with his neighbor, for we are members one of another." Truthfulness is a hallmark of integrity, as it reflects a commitment to honesty and transparency in all interactions. Whether in personal relationships, business dealings, or public life, a person of integrity is known for their truthfulness and reliability.

In addition to truthfulness, integrity involves consistency. James 1:22 again emphasizes the importance of aligning our actions with our beliefs: "But be doers of the word, and not hearers only, deceiving yourselves." A person of integrity does not merely profess their faith but lives it out in every area of life. This consistency is evident in how they treat others, how they handle money, how they respond to challenges, and how they make decisions.

Furthermore, integrity requires courage. It often takes courage to stand up for what is right, especially when it is unpopular or comes with personal cost. Joshua 1:9 again offers encouragement: "Have I not commanded you? Be strong and courageous. Do not be frightened, and do not be dismayed, for Jehovah your God is with you wherever you go." Courage is essential for maintaining integrity, as it enables us to resist the pressures and temptations that might lead us astray.

Finally, integrity is sustained through accountability. Proverbs 27:17 again observes, "Iron sharpens iron, and one man sharpens another." Having relationships with fellow believers who hold us accountable and encourage us in our walk with Jehovah is vital for maintaining integrity. These relationships provide support, guidance, and correction, helping us stay on the path of righteousness.

Moral Integrity Is Essential

Moral integrity is not just a desirable quality; it is essential for anyone who seeks to live a life that honors Jehovah. Without integrity, our faith is hollow, and our witness to the world is compromised. 1 Peter 2:12 again urges believers, "Keep your conduct among the Gentiles honorable, so that when they speak against you as evildoers, they may see your good deeds and glorify God on the day of visitation." Our integrity serves as a testimony to others, pointing them to the transforming power of God's grace.

Moral integrity involves more than just avoiding obvious sins; it requires a commitment to holiness in every area of life. 1 Peter 1:15-16 again calls believers to this standard: "But as he who called you is holy, you also be holy in all your conduct, since it is written, 'You shall be holy, for I am holy.'" Holiness is not an option for the believer; it is a command. To walk in integrity, we must strive for holiness, seeking to reflect God's character in all that we do.

Integrity also has a profound impact on our relationships. Proverbs 22:1 again states, "A good name is to be chosen rather than great riches, and favor is better than silver or gold." Our reputation is built on the foundation of integrity, and it influences how others perceive and trust us. A person of integrity is respected, trusted, and admired, while a person who lacks integrity is often viewed with suspicion and distrust.

Moreover, integrity is crucial for effective leadership. Proverbs 29:2 again observes, "When the righteous increase, the people rejoice, but when the wicked rule, the people groan." Leaders who possess integrity inspire confidence and loyalty in those they lead. They make decisions based on what is right, not what is expedient, and they are willing to stand by their principles even when it is difficult. In contrast, leaders who lack integrity often make decisions based on selfish interests, leading to corruption and injustice.

Moral integrity is also a source of inner strength and peace. Isaiah 26:3 again promises, "You keep him in perfect peace whose mind is stayed on you, because he trusts in you." When we walk in integrity, we experience the peace that comes from knowing we are living in alignment with God's will. This peace is not dependent on external circumstances but is rooted in our relationship with Jehovah.

Finally, moral integrity is essential for eternal life. Revelation 21:27 again describes the New Jerusalem, saying, "But nothing unclean will ever enter it, nor anyone who does what is detestable or false, but only those who are written in the Lamb's book of life." Only those who have walked in integrity, who have been cleansed by the blood of Christ, will enter into the fullness of eternal life with Jehovah. Therefore, integrity is not just a matter of earthly conduct; it has eternal significance.

Be Exemplary in Dealing with Others

One of the key areas where integrity must be demonstrated is in our dealings with others. This includes how we interact with family,

PUT OFF THE OLD PERSON

friends, colleagues, and even strangers. Colossians 3:23-24 again instructs, "Whatever you do, work heartily, as for the Lord and not for men, knowing that from the Lord you will receive the inheritance as your reward. You are serving the Lord Christ." In every interaction, we are ultimately serving Jehovah, and our conduct should reflect His character.

Being exemplary in dealing with others means treating everyone with respect, kindness, and fairness. James 2:1 again warns against showing partiality: "My brothers, show no partiality as you hold the faith in our Lord Jesus Christ, the Lord of glory." Integrity requires that we treat all people with dignity and honor, regardless of their status, background, or relationship to us. This includes being honest and transparent in our communications, fulfilling our promises, and acting with fairness in all our dealings.

Moreover, integrity in relationships involves maintaining healthy boundaries and avoiding actions that could harm others. Romans 13:10 again reminds us, "Love does no wrong to a neighbor; therefore love is the fulfilling of the law." Love is the guiding principle for all our interactions, and it requires us to act in ways that build up others rather than tear them down. This includes avoiding gossip, slander, and other forms of harmful speech, as well as being faithful and trustworthy in all our commitments.

In the workplace, integrity involves doing our work with excellence and honesty, even when no one is watching. Proverbs 11:1 again declares, "A false balance is an abomination to Jehovah, but a just weight is his delight." This verse speaks to the importance of honesty and fairness in business dealings. Whether we are employees, employers, or business owners, our conduct in the workplace should be marked by integrity, reflecting the values of God's kingdom.

In our families, integrity means being faithful to our commitments and modeling Christlike behavior to our spouses, children, and extended family members. Ephesians 6:4 again instructs fathers, "Do not provoke your children to anger, but bring them up in the discipline and instruction of the Lord." Integrity in parenting involves being consistent, loving, and fair in how we discipline and instruct our children. It also means being a role model of godly character, showing our children what it looks like to live a life of integrity.

In our communities, integrity requires us to be good citizens, obeying the laws of the land, and contributing to the well-being of society. Romans 13:1 again exhorts, "Let every person be subject to the governing authorities. For there is no authority except from God, and those that exist have been instituted by God." While there may be times when we must stand against unjust laws or practices, in general, we are called to be law-abiding citizens who seek the common good. This includes being involved in our communities in ways that promote justice, mercy, and truth.

Hold Firmly to True Worship

Integrity is also closely tied to our worship of Jehovah. True worship is not just about performing religious rituals or attending church services; it is about living a life that is fully devoted to God. John 4:24 again teaches, "God is spirit, and those who worship him must worship in spirit and truth." True worship involves both the heart and the mind, aligning our entire being with God's will.

Holding firmly to true worship means rejecting idolatry in all its forms. Exodus 20:3-5 again commands, "You shall have no other gods before me. You shall not make for yourself a carved image, or any likeness of anything that is in heaven above, or that is in the earth beneath, or that is in the water under the earth. You shall not bow down to them or serve them, for I Jehovah your God am a jealous God." Idolatry is not just about worshiping statues or images; it includes anything that takes the place of God in our hearts, whether it be money, power, relationships, or self.

True worship also involves a commitment to purity and holiness. James 1:27 again defines pure religion: "Religion that is pure and undefiled before God, the Father, is this: to visit orphans and widows in their affliction, and to keep oneself unstained from the world." Integrity in worship requires that we keep ourselves free from the moral corruption of the world, living in a way that is distinct and set apart for Jehovah.

Furthermore, true worship requires consistency between our public and private lives. Matthew 6:1 again warns, "Beware of practicing your righteousness before other people in order to be seen by them, for then you will have no reward from your Father who is in heaven." Integrity in worship means that our devotion to God is not just a show for others; it is genuine and sincere, whether we are in the public eye or alone with God.

Holding firmly to true worship also involves being faithful to the teachings of Scripture. 2 Timothy 4:2-4 again charges believers, "Preach the word; be ready in season and out of season; reprove, rebuke, and exhort, with complete patience and teaching. For the time is coming when people will not endure sound teaching, but having itching ears they will accumulate for themselves teachers to suit their own passions, and will turn away from listening to the truth and wander off into myths." In a world where false teachings and distortions of the gospel are prevalent, maintaining integrity in worship means holding fast to the truth of God's Word and rejecting any teaching that deviates from it.

Finally, integrity in worship means that our lives are a living sacrifice to God. Romans 12:1 again exhorts, "I appeal to you therefore, brothers, by the mercies of God, to present your bodies as a living sacrifice, holy and acceptable to God, which is your spiritual worship." Our worship is not confined to a specific time or place; it is expressed in every aspect of our lives, as we offer ourselves wholly to God in service and obedience.

Edward D. Andrews

CHAPTER 13 How Can We Build a Successful and Godly Family Life?

Understanding and Appreciating Your Role in the Family

Family life is one of the most significant areas where Christian values are tested and displayed. In the family, each member has a unique role that, when understood and appreciated, contributes to the overall success and harmony of the household. The Bible provides clear guidance on the roles of husbands, wives, and children, emphasizing the importance of love, respect, and mutual submission.

Husbands are called to lead their families with love and care, reflecting Christ's relationship with the Church. Ephesians 5:25 instructs, "Husbands, love your wives, as Christ loved the church and gave himself up for her." This command underscores the sacrificial nature of a husband's love, which prioritizes the well-being of his wife and family above his own desires. A husband who leads with love and integrity sets the tone for the entire household, creating an environment where each member can thrive.

Wives are called to support their husbands and manage the household with wisdom and grace. Proverbs 31:10-12 praises the virtuous wife: "An excellent wife who can find? She is far more precious than jewels. The heart of her husband trusts in her, and he will have no lack of gain. She does him good, and not harm, all the days of her life." A wife who embraces her role with joy and diligence contributes significantly to the success of the family, ensuring that the home is a place of peace and order.

Children are instructed to obey and honor their parents. Ephesians 6:1-3 commands, "Children, obey your parents in the Lord, for this is right. 'Honor your father and mother' (this is the first commandment with a promise), 'that it may go well with you and that you may live long in the land.'" Obedience to parents is a key aspect of a child's role in the family, and it is closely linked to the promise of a blessed life. When children understand and fulfill their role, they contribute to the overall harmony and success of the family.

In addition to these specific roles, all family members are called to live out the Christian virtues of love, patience, kindness, and forgiveness. Colossians 3:12-14 again encourages believers, "Put on then, as God's chosen ones, holy and beloved, compassionate hearts, kindness, humility, meekness, and patience, bearing with one another and, if one has a complaint against another, forgiving each other; as Jehovah has forgiven you, so you also must forgive. And above all these put on love, which binds everything together in perfect harmony." When each member of the family strives to embody these virtues, the family becomes a reflection of God's love and grace.

Commitment: The Foundation of a Strong Marriage

A successful family life begins with a strong and committed marriage. Commitment is the foundation upon which a marriage is built, and it requires both spouses to be fully dedicated to one another and to the vows they made before God. Malachi 2:14-16 again speaks to the seriousness of the marriage covenant: "But you say, 'Why does he not?' Because Jehovah was witness between you and the wife of your youth, to whom you have been faithless, though she is your companion and your wife by covenant. Did he not make them one, with a portion of the Spirit in their union? And what was the one God seeking? Godly offspring. So guard yourselves in your spirit, and let none of you be faithless to the wife of your youth." Marriage is not just a human institution; it is a sacred covenant that reflects the unity and faithfulness of God.

Three practical tips can help marriage mates stay together:

Prioritize Your Relationship: In the busyness of life, it is easy for spouses to drift apart. However, it is essential to make time for one another, nurturing the relationship through regular communication, shared activities, and expressions of love. Ecclesiastes 4:9-12 again reminds us of the strength that comes from unity: "Two are better than one, because they have a good reward for their toil. For if they fall, one will lift up his fellow. But woe to him who is alone when he falls and has not another to lift him up! Again, if two lie together, they keep warm, but how can one keep warm alone? And though a man might prevail against one who is alone, two will withstand him—a threefold cord is not quickly broken."

Practice Forgiveness: No marriage is without its challenges, and spouses will inevitably hurt each other at times. Forgiveness is essential for maintaining a strong and healthy marriage. Ephesians 4:32 again encourages, "Be kind to one another, tenderhearted, forgiving one another, as God in Christ forgave you." Forgiveness allows spouses to move past hurts and continue building a loving relationship.

Seek God's Guidance Together: A marriage that is grounded in a shared faith in Jehovah is one that can withstand the storms of life. Proverbs 3:5-6 again advises, "Trust in Jehovah with all your heart, and do not lean on your own understanding. In all your ways acknowledge him, and he will make straight your paths." By seeking Jehovah's guidance together, spouses can navigate the challenges of life with wisdom and strength.

Teamwork: Strengthening the Marriage Partnership

Marriage is a partnership, and like any partnership, it requires teamwork to succeed. Ecclesiastes 4:9-12 again emphasizes the importance of working together: "Two are better than one, because they have a good reward for their toil. For if they fall, one will lift up his fellow." In marriage, teamwork means supporting one another in all areas of life, whether in parenting, managing the household, or pursuing shared goals.

Does your marriage mate seem more like a roommate? This question is a common concern for many couples, especially as the years go by and the demands of life increase. When spouses begin to feel like roommates rather than partners, it is often a sign that the marriage has become transactional rather than relational. To rekindle the partnership, couples need to focus on building intimacy and connection.

Intimacy in marriage goes beyond physical closeness; it includes emotional, spiritual, and intellectual connection. Ephesians 5:31 again recalls the Genesis account: "Therefore a man shall leave his father and mother and hold fast to his wife, and the two shall become one flesh." This oneness encompasses all aspects of the relationship and requires intentional effort to maintain.

Practical steps to strengthen the partnership include:

Shared Experiences: Engage in activities that you both enjoy, whether it's a hobby, a sport, or simply spending time together. These shared experiences build memories and deepen your connection.

Open Communication: Talk about your hopes, dreams, and concerns. Proverbs 18:13 again warns, "If one gives an answer before he hears, it is his folly and shame." Listening and understanding your spouse's perspective fosters mutual respect and unity.

Spiritual Growth Together: Pray together, study the Bible, and attend worship services as a couple. Matthew 18:20 again promises, "For where two or three are gathered in my name, there am I among them." Spiritual unity strengthens the bond between spouses and keeps Jehovah at the center of the marriage.

Respect: The Pillar of a Healthy Marriage

Respect is a fundamental aspect of any successful marriage. Without respect, love cannot thrive, and the marriage relationship becomes strained. Ephesians 5:33 again instructs, "However, let each one of you love his wife as himself, and let the wife see that she respects her husband." This mutual respect is essential for a healthy and harmonious marriage.

Learn what words and actions are essential to ensure that your spouse feels respected. Respect in marriage involves both what we say and what we do. Words have the power to build up or tear down, and spouses must be mindful of how they speak to one another. Proverbs 15:1 again teaches, "A soft answer turns away wrath, but a harsh word stirs up anger." Gentle and kind speech fosters respect and understanding in the marriage relationship.

Actions also speak volumes. Respect is demonstrated through acts of consideration, support, and honor. Romans 12:10 again encourages, "Love one another with brotherly affection. Outdo one another in showing honor." When spouses go out of their way to honor and serve each other, they strengthen the bonds of respect and love.

Practical ways to show respect in marriage include:

Active Listening: Give your spouse your full attention when they speak, showing that you value their thoughts and feelings. James 1:19 again advises, "Know this, my beloved brothers: let every person be quick to hear, slow to speak, slow to anger."

Supporting Their Interests: Take an interest in your spouse's hobbies and passions, even if they differ from your own. Philippians 2:4 again encourages, "Let each of you look not only to his own interests, but also to the interests of others."

Respecting Their Boundaries: Every individual has personal boundaries, and respecting these boundaries is crucial for maintaining mutual respect in marriage. 1 Corinthians 13:5 again describes love as "not rude. It does not insist on its own way; it is not irritable or resentful."

Forgiveness: The Healing Balm for Marriage

Forgiveness is an essential component of a successful marriage. No matter how strong a marriage may be, there will be times when one spouse hurts the other, whether intentionally or unintentionally. Colossians 3:13 again instructs, "bearing with one another and, if one has a complaint against another, forgiving each other; as Jehovah has forgiven you, so you also must forgive." Forgiveness allows couples to move past offenses and continue building a loving relationship.

What can help you see past your mate's imperfections? Recognizing that we are all imperfect and in need of grace can help us extend forgiveness to our spouse. Romans 3:23 again reminds us, "for all have sinned and fall short of the glory of God." When we understand our own need for forgiveness, we are more likely to forgive others.

Forgiveness in marriage is not just about letting go of past hurts; it is about choosing to love and cherish your spouse despite their imperfections. 1 Corinthians 13:7 again describes love as "bears all things, believes all things, hopes all things, endures all things." This kind of love is patient and willing to overlook faults, focusing instead on the positive qualities of the spouse.

Practical steps to cultivate forgiveness in marriage include:

Acknowledge the Hurt: Before forgiveness can occur, it is important to acknowledge the hurt and discuss it openly. Ephesians 4:26 again advises, "Be angry and do not sin; do not let the sun go down on your anger." Addressing issues promptly prevents resentment from taking root.

Choose to Forgive: Forgiveness is a choice, not a feeling. It involves a conscious decision to release the offense and not hold it against the other person. Matthew 6:14-15 again teaches, "For if you forgive others their trespasses, your heavenly Father will also forgive you, but if you do not forgive others their trespasses, neither will your Father forgive your trespasses."

Seek Reconciliation: Forgiveness should lead to reconciliation, where the relationship is restored and strengthened. Romans 12:18 again exhorts, "If possible, so far as it depends on you, live peaceably with all."

Communication: The Key to Understanding and Connection

Effective communication is vital for a successful family life. Without clear and open communication, misunderstandings arise, leading to conflict and disconnection. Proverbs 18:21 again highlights the power of words: "Death and life are in the power of the tongue, and those who love it will eat its fruits." The words we speak have the power to build up or tear down, and in a family setting, this power is magnified.

Three key steps can help you to draw closer to your children and improve communication within the family:

Active Listening: Children, like adults, need to feel heard and understood. James 1:19 again advises, "Know this, my beloved brothers: let every person be quick to hear, slow to speak, slow to anger." When parents take the time to listen actively to their children, they foster a sense of trust and connection. This involves not only hearing the words but also understanding the emotions and concerns behind them.

Open and Honest Dialogue: Encourage open and honest communication within the family by creating an environment where everyone feels safe to express their thoughts and feelings. Ephesians 4:25 again instructs, "Therefore, having put away falsehood, let each one of you speak the truth with his neighbor, for we are members one of another." Honesty and transparency are key to building strong relationships.

Positive Reinforcement: Use words to encourage and uplift your children, rather than criticize or belittle them. Proverbs 16:24 again teaches, "Gracious words are like a honeycomb, sweetness to the soul and health to the body." Positive reinforcement helps to build your children's self-esteem and encourages them to communicate more openly.

Practical steps for effective communication within the family include:

Regular Family Meetings: Set aside time each week for a family meeting where everyone can share their thoughts, concerns, and ideas. This helps to keep communication lines open and ensures that everyone feels heard.

Daily Check-ins: Make it a habit to check in with each family member daily, even if it's just for a few minutes. This helps to maintain a strong connection and allows for ongoing communication.

Conflict Resolution: Teach your children healthy ways to resolve conflicts, such as talking things out, finding a compromise, and apologizing when necessary. Matthew 5:9 again blesses peacemakers: "Blessed are the peacemakers, for they shall be called sons of God." By modeling and teaching these skills, you help your children develop strong communication and relational skills.

Discipline of Children: Guiding Them with Love and Consistency

Discipline is an essential aspect of parenting, but it must be done with love and consistency. Proverbs 13:24 again advises, "Whoever spares the rod hates his son, but he who loves him is diligent to discipline him." Discipline is not about punishment; it is about teaching and guiding children to make wise choices and develop godly character.

Does discipline undermine a child's self-esteem? No, when done correctly, discipline actually builds a child's self-esteem by providing clear boundaries and expectations. Hebrews 12:11 again acknowledges, "For the moment all discipline seems painful rather than pleasant, but later it yields the peaceful fruit of righteousness to those who have been trained by it." Discipline, when applied with love and consistency, helps children feel secure and confident.

Be consistent. Be reasonable. Be loving. These three principles are key to effective discipline. Consistency ensures that children understand the rules and the consequences for breaking them. Ephesians 6:4 again instructs fathers, "Do not provoke your children to anger, but bring them up in the discipline and instruction of the Lord." Reasonableness ensures that the discipline is appropriate for the child's age and the severity of the offense. Love ensures that the discipline is motivated by a desire to help the child grow, rather than by anger or frustration.

Physical spanking off a few firm swats to the butt is not abusive but only to get the child's attention so as to listen. Proverbs 22:15 again teaches, "Folly is bound up in the heart of a child, but the rod of discipline drives it far from him." While physical discipline should be used sparingly and only as a last resort, it can be effective in getting a child's attention and reinforcing the seriousness of their actions. However, it must always be done in love and never in anger.

Practical steps for effective discipline include:

Set Clear Expectations: Make sure your children understand the rules and the consequences for breaking them. This helps to prevent misunderstandings and ensures that the discipline is fair.

Follow Through: Be consistent in enforcing the rules. If a consequence is given, make sure it is carried out. This teaches children that their actions have consequences and helps them develop self-discipline.

Use Positive Reinforcement: In addition to discipline, use positive reinforcement to encourage good behavior. Proverbs 11:30 again reminds us, "The fruit of the righteous is a tree of life, and whoever captures souls is wise." By rewarding good behavior, you reinforce the values and behaviors you want to see in your children.

Values: Teaching Your Children What Matters Most

As parents, one of the most important responsibilities is to teach your children the values that will guide their lives. Deuteronomy 6:6-7 again instructs, "And these words that I command you today shall be on your heart. You shall teach them diligently to your children, and shall talk of them when you sit in your house, and when you walk by the way, and when you lie down, and when you rise." Teaching values is not just about giving instructions; it is about modeling those values in your own life and making them a part of your daily conversations.

What standards should you teach your children? The Bible provides a clear set of standards that should be at the heart of your child's upbringing. These include:

PUT OFF THE OLD PERSON

Love for Jehovah: Matthew 22:37 again instructs, "You shall love Jehovah your God with all your heart and with all your soul and with all your mind." Teaching your children to love and serve Jehovah is the foundation of all other values.

Respect for Others: Matthew 7:12 again teaches, "So whatever you wish that others would do to you, do also to them, for this is the Law and the Prophets." Respect for others is a key value that should be instilled in children from a young age.

Honesty: Proverbs 12:22 again says, "Lying lips are an abomination to Jehovah, but those who act faithfully are his delight." Teaching your children the importance of honesty and integrity will help them build strong relationships and a good reputation.

Kindness and Compassion: Ephesians 4:32 again encourages, "Be kind to one another, tenderhearted, forgiving one another, as God in Christ forgave you." Kindness and compassion should be modeled and taught as essential Christian values.

Hard Work and Responsibility: Colossians 3:23-24 again instructs, "Whatever you do, work heartily, as for the Lord and not for men, knowing that from the Lord you will receive the inheritance as your reward." Teaching your children the value of hard work and responsibility will prepare them for success in life.

Practical ways to teach values to your children include:

Model the Values: Children learn by watching their parents. Make sure that your actions are in line with the values you are teaching.

Discuss Values Regularly: Use everyday situations to discuss values with your children. Whether it's a news story, a TV show, or something that happened at school, these can be opportunities to talk about what is right and wrong.

Reinforce Values with Scripture: Use Bible verses to reinforce the values you are teaching. Psalm 119:11 again says, "I have stored up your word in my heart, that I might not sin against you." Teaching your children to rely on Scripture as their guide helps to instill these values deeply in their hearts.

Example: Leading by Example in the Home

As the saying goes, "Actions speak louder than words." In the home, the example set by the parents is one of the most powerful teaching tools available. 1 Timothy 4:12 again advises, "Let no one despise you for your youth, but set the believers an example in speech, in conduct, in love, in faith, in purity." This principle applies not only to youth but to all believers, especially parents.

If you want your words to reach your children, they must be in harmony with your actions. Children are quick to notice when there is a disconnect between what their parents say and what they do. If parents preach honesty but are not truthful themselves, or if they talk about the importance of kindness but are harsh and unkind in their behavior, children will quickly learn to dismiss what they hear. James 1:22 again warns, "But be doers of the word, and not hearers only, deceiving yourselves." To effectively teach your children, your actions must align with your words.

Practical ways to lead by example include:

Consistency in Behavior: Ensure that your behavior reflects the values you are teaching. If you value honesty, be truthful in all your dealings. If you value kindness, be kind in your interactions with others.

Admit Mistakes: When you fail to live up to the standards you are teaching, be honest about it with your children. Apologize and use it as a teaching moment to show them how to handle mistakes with integrity.

Involve Your Children in Service: Model a life of service by involving your children in acts of kindness and service to others. This could include volunteering at a local charity, helping a neighbor, or simply showing hospitality to others.

Identity: Helping Your Children Stand Firm in Their Faith

In a world that is increasingly hostile to Christian values, helping your children stand firm in their faith is more important than ever. Ephesians 6:10-11 again exhorts, "Finally, be strong in Jehovah and in the strength of his might. Put on the whole armor of God, that you may be able to stand against the schemes of the devil." Equipping your children with a strong sense of identity in Christ is essential for helping them navigate the challenges they will face.

How can young people stand up for their Christian beliefs? Young people face tremendous pressure to conform to the world around them, but they can stand firm in their faith by grounding their identity in Christ. Galatians 2:20 again declares, "I have been crucified with Christ. It is no longer I who live, but Christ who lives in me. And the life I now live in the flesh I live by faith in the Son of God, who loved me and gave himself for me." When young people understand that their identity is found in Christ, they are better equipped to resist the pressures of the world.

Practical steps to help your children stand firm in their faith include:

Teach Them Who They Are in Christ: Help your children understand that their primary identity is as a child of God. Romans 8:16-17 again reassures, "The Spirit himself bears witness with our spirit that we are children of God, and if children, then heirs—heirs of God and fellow heirs with Christ, provided we suffer with him in order that we may also be glorified with him."

Encourage Them to Stand Firm in Their Beliefs: Teach your children to stand up for their beliefs, even when it is difficult. 1 Corinthians 16:13 again commands, "Be watchful, stand firm in the faith, act like men, be strong."

Provide a Supportive Community: Surround your children with other believers who can support and encourage them in their faith. Hebrews 10:24-25 again exhorts, "And let us consider how to stir up one another to love and good works, not neglecting to meet together, as is the habit of some, but encouraging one another, and all the more as you see the Day drawing near."

Trustworthiness: Building Trust in the Parent-Child Relationship

Trust is the foundation of any strong relationship, and this is especially true in the parent-child relationship. Proverbs 3:5-6 again advises, "Trust in Jehovah with all your heart, and do not lean on your own understanding. In all your ways acknowledge him, and he will make straight your paths." Building trust with your children involves being reliable, consistent, and honest in your interactions with them.

Earning your parent's trust is an important step in becoming an adult. As children grow, they need to learn how to take on more responsibility and make decisions for themselves. Trust is a key component of this process. When children earn their parents' trust, they gain more freedom and responsibility, which helps them mature into responsible adults.

Practical steps to build trust with your children include:

Be Consistent: Follow through on your promises and be consistent in your expectations. This helps your children know what to expect and builds their confidence in your reliability.

Give Them Responsibility: Allow your children to take on age-appropriate responsibilities and trust them to follow through. This helps them develop a sense of responsibility and builds trust in their ability to handle tasks.

Be Honest: Be open and honest with your children, even when it's difficult. Honesty fosters trust and sets a positive example for your children to follow.

Industriousness: Instilling a Strong Work Ethic

A strong work ethic is an essential value that will serve your children well throughout their lives. Proverbs 12:11 again teaches,

"Whoever works his land will have plenty of bread, but he who follows worthless pursuits lacks sense." Instilling a sense of industriousness in your children helps them understand the value of hard work and prepares them for success in all areas of life.

Learning how to work hard as a youth can help you to be successful at whatever you do in life. When children learn the value of hard work at a young age, they develop skills and habits that will benefit them in their future careers, relationships, and personal pursuits. Colossians 3:23 again instructs, "Whatever you do, work heartily, as for the Lord and not for men." Teaching your children to work hard is not just about preparing them for a job; it's about helping them develop character and discipline.

Practical steps to instill a strong work ethic in your children include:

Assign Chores and Responsibilities: Give your children regular chores and responsibilities around the house. This teaches them the value of contributing to the family and helps them develop a sense of responsibility.

Set Goals and Encourage Perseverance: Help your children set goals for themselves, whether it's in school, sports, or personal pursuits. Encourage them to work hard and persevere until they achieve their goals.

Praise Effort, Not Just Results: Praise your children for their hard work and effort, not just for the results they achieve. This helps them understand that the process is just as important as the outcome.

Goals: Helping Your Children Set and Achieve Their Goals

Setting and achieving goals is an important part of personal growth and development. Proverbs 16:3 again advises, "Commit your work to Jehovah, and your plans will be established." Helping your children set and achieve goals teaches them the importance of planning, perseverance, and discipline.

Reaching goals can boost your confidence, strengthen your friendships, and increase your happiness. When children achieve their goals, they gain a sense of accomplishment and confidence. This not only benefits them personally but also strengthens their relationships with others and contributes to their overall happiness. Philippians 3:13-14 again encourages, "Brothers, I do not consider that I have made it my own. But one thing I do: forgetting what lies behind and straining forward to what lies ahead, I press on toward the goal for the prize of the upward call of God in Christ Jesus." Setting and pursuing goals helps children develop a forward-looking mindset, focused on growth and improvement.

Practical steps to help your children set and achieve goals include:

Help Them Identify Their Interests and Passions: Encourage your children to explore their interests and passions, and help them set goals that align with these areas. This increases their motivation and commitment to achieving their goals.

Teach Them to Break Down Goals into Manageable Steps: Help your children break down their goals into smaller, manageable steps. This makes the goals more achievable and helps them stay on track.

Celebrate Their Achievements: Celebrate your children's achievements, no matter how small. This reinforces their hard work and encourages them to continue setting and pursuing goals.

www.ingramcontent.com/pod-product-compliance
Lightning Source LLC
LaVergne TN
LVHW020932090426
835512LV00020B/3326